CW01081752

QUEERING YOU
PRACTICE

Queering Your Therapy Practice: Queer Theory, Narrative Therapy, and Imagining New Identities is the first practice-based book for therapists that presents queer theory and narrative therapy as praxis allies.

This book offers fresh, hopeful resources for therapists committed to culturally responsive work with queer and trans people, and the important others in their lives. It features clinical vignettes from the author's practice that bring to life the application of queer theory through the practice of narrative therapy and serve as teaching tools for the specific concepts and practices highlighted in individual, relational, and family therapy contexts. The text also weaves in questions for reflection and discussion, and Q-tips summarizing key points and practices.

A practical resource for both seasoned therapists and students, Queering Your Therapy Practice demonstrates how therapeutic practice can be informed, improved, and deepened by queer theory.

Julie Tilsen, PhD (she/her/hers), is a therapist, consultant, and trainer, and the author of Narrative Approaches to Youth Work and Therapeutic Conversations with Queer Youth. She is based in the USA.

QUEERING YOUR THERAPY PRACTICE

Queer Theory, Narrative Therapy, and
Imagining New Identities

Julie Tilsen

NEW YORK AND LONDON

First published 2021
by Routledge
52 Vanderbilt Avenue, New York, NY 10017

and by Routledge
2 Park Square, Milton Park, Abingdon, Oxon, OX14 4RN

Routledge is an imprint of the Taylor & Francis Group, an informa business

Library of Congress Cataloging-in-Publication Data
A catalog record for this title has been requested

ISBN: 978-0-367-82019-0 (hbk)
ISBN: 978-0-367-82020-6 (pbk)
ISBN: 978-1-003-01147-7 (ebk)

Typeset in Joanna
by codeMantra

CONTENTS

FOREWORD

Stories about us have already been told, even before we take our first breath into this world. There are stories about how we came to exist, whether we will be welcomed warmly or not, and stories about expectations that our caregivers have of who we might become. Our names sometimes carry the stories of those who have gone before in our own family lines. We might even share the name of another older, living family member. We come into the world surrounded by stories, carrying their weight, being shaped by them until we are old enough to tell our own stories and to evaluate the stories we were given to decide what still fits and what needs to be composted and left behind.

These stories are not just familial and personal; they are also cultural, historical, and social. They depend on our geographical location; the language(s) we are born into; the social positions our family members and we occupy; and the ways our bodies are racialized and categorized in relation to class, standards of health, and more. Stories have power, and, some would say, they are the currency of therapy. In *Queering Your Therapy Practice*, Julie Tilsen guides us to understand not only why stories are important but also how language shapes us and our relationships. She does not shy away from a critical analysis of the power of dominant discourses. Julie tackles the gargantuan task of making accessible complex and fluid theoretical ideas, such as queer theory and narrative therapy, so that they can be applied to our everyday practices as clinicians.

Even though I am a writer, as well as a family therapist, sex therapist, and clinical supervisor, I struggled to find the words to describe just how important and groundbreaking this book is. Julie takes several matters that are close to my heart—such as systemic thinking, queer theories, narrative practices, and working with marginalized clients— and weaves them seamlessly into a book that should be recommended reading for anyone who has ever sat with a client or anyone who is planning on sitting with a client. In fact, even though the book is aimed at colleagues within the mental health field, the tapestry woven so expertly in this book would also benefit educators and allied health professionals. Hopefully, you can understand why it has been so challenging for me to find words to describe how vital this book is to our field.

To better illustrate why I believe this book is such a vital contribution to the therapeutic field, let me get personal for a few moments. One of the stories I was born into five decades ago is that I was assigned female at birth and assumed to be straight in a predominantly Catholic country. I had no words or frameworks for many of my feelings and experiences growing up, and I started to find them in another language after I had migrated away from everything familiar: land, family, friends, and community. It was through geographical and linguistic displacement that I came to name myself as bi, trans, queer, and nonbinary. With time, I also came to understand my story as one of displacement from home, in great part due to my own trans and queer identities. It would take books to unpack all of these stories; so, for now, suffice it to say that several of these stories included painful encounters with clinical providers and, later, with educators and clinical supervisors.

The first time I ever sought out counseling support, in fact, I was told that maybe, if I were willing to take on more feminine endeavors, such as knitting or baking, maybe I would not have so much conflict with one of the cis, white, Anglo professors in my PhD program. At times, I believe it is a genuine miracle that I ever sought therapeutic support again. Or maybe it was just a desperate need for support and understanding! That counselor needed this book. She needed to understand how patriarchy and gender were impacting me. She needed to uncouple gender from wonderful activities, such as knitting and baking, which I very much enjoy, by the way. If she had had the skills to invite me into queering her own and my understanding of what was happening in my life, I would have been spared a few years of strife! Dr. Tilsen could have shown her how a praxis that combines queer theories and narrative therapy can be liberatory and far more ethical than what happened to me in that therapy room in the mid-1990s.

Not long after that, I found my way to what Julie calls the *audacity of queerness*, as I embraced and embodied my intersecting identities. However, when I started my education to become a therapist, the power of normative discourses continued to weigh heavily on me. I was told that I would never be a therapist if I did not want to train in a psychodynamic approach. Even when I chose a systemic-oriented training program with a significant narrative therapy component, there was not much space for queerness, let alone a trans identity. Dominant discourse dictates that people like me were never meant to be the therapist in the room, only the client. Yet, even though my program was not as ready for all the intersections I embodied, narrative therapy showed me the possibility of developing a counter narrative, a new story, in which I could have the audacity to be queer, trans, disabled, an immigrant... and a therapist. In fact, I became so audacious, I now hold multiple specialty certifications, serve as a clinical supervisor, and contribute to scholarship in our field.

This is why I want every therapist, psychologist, counselor, psychiatrist, and educator in these fields and beyond to read *Queering Your Therapy Practice*. This is the book I wanted every one of my past therapists to have read, the book I wanted to read as a student, and the book I will now have the pleasure of recommending to each student and supervisee I come into contact with. Thank you for picking up this book and choosing to enrich your clinical practice. I know that whether you are a new or seasoned clinician, familiar with queer theories or not, competent in narrative therapy or not, there is a precious thread in this book for you, a thread that you and all your clients will benefit from.

Happy reading.

Alex Iantaffi, PhD, MS, SEP, CST, LMFT
Author of *How to Understand Your
Gender*, *Life Isn't Binary*, and *Gender Trauma*

ACKNOWLEDGMENTS

Gratitude is when memory is stored in the heart and not in the mind. – Lionel Hampton

My heart is filled with memories of so many who helped me out with this book through their unforgettable generosity:

To the Dakota and Ojibwe peoples, upon whose stolen lands I live and write, I acknowledge your ongoing stewardship and protection of the land.

To the queer and trans elders and ancestors, activists, organizers, artists, scholars, agitators, resisters, poets, survivors, writers, martyrs, and wonderers, I am grateful to be standing on your shoulders.

To my editors at Routledge, Clare Ashworth and Heather Evans, and editorial assistant Ellie Duncan, much appreciation for your gentle guidance with and strong support of this book.

To my agent/editor and favorite brother-in-law Scott Edelstein, thanks for doing the things-that-must-be-done-but-I-don't-do to make sure this book happens.

To Kandace Creel Falcón and Liz Kuoppala and The Goats, thank you for making available your sweet space so I could begin this writing journey in such a special place. I don't think I can ever write again without the inspiration of goats and the beauty of Otter Tail County, Minnesota.

To Alex Flip, my appreciation for your critically queer thoughtfulness about professional ethics and your support of my work.

To Kristen Benson, Sheila McNamee, and Dave Nylund (my triumvirate of loving and supportive friends who are all such wicked smart scholars and amazing writers), there's an entire chamber of my heart filled with gratitude for your feedback on various components and iterations of the manuscript. Also, big thanks for the bottomless cup of encouragement you each served up during this entire process.

To Katie Heiden Rootes, unending appreciation for reading EVERY DAMN WORD I wrote to make sure it was worth reading. Everyone should have a friend who cares that much *and* knows what the hell she's talking about. Katie, my beer is your beer.

To Alex Iantaffi, big thanks and big love for writing such a heart-full foreword for this undertaking and for blazing plenty of queered trails in your own work and scholarship.

To all those who, for 30 years, have invited me into your lives as your therapist, supervisor, or teacher, thank you for your grace, patience, and trust. Your stories live in my heart as invitations to your wisdom fostered through humility and struggle; your fierce queerness, embodied as resistance, humor, and undeterred resolve; and your hope and wonderment at what *could be*. My time with each of you is a gift of immeasurable value.

To Lauri, "thank you" doesn't do the work here that needs to be done to convey the truth that there is no book without you. Let's ride this thing out together, my love.

INTRODUCTION

Preparing a Path for the Unicorn

Mic, a 13-year-old expert on all things Harry Potter, sighed, shook their[1] head, looked at me through tears, and said, "You know, it's not like everyone at school attends the GSA.[2] Not everyone learns about the gender unicorn, not even all the teachers. I'm tired of having to explain all the time. I don't even need them to agree, or even understand everything, but can't they just respect what I tell them? It just sucks."

Mic is a white, gender non-binary young person frustrated with the effects of living in a world organized by the gender binary. As I listen to their hurt and exasperation, a cartoon unicorn trots across the marquee of my mind's eye.

"Mic, I'm really sorry that this sucks so much. I get that it's really hard, and you're doing everything you can." I paused. "I have a goofy question. Is it OK to ask now, or is there more you wanted to say about how much this all sucks?"

"Your goofy questions usually help when things suck, so OK, go ahead."

"Mic, if the gender unicorn were to trot in here, burping rainbows and throwing glitter everywhere, and it made the idea of male and female, gay and straight, and all the rules and assumptions that go with those things disappear, what would happen? What would that make possible?"

I watch a smile slowly crawl across Mic's face, even as tears make tracks to the corners of their mouth.

"If the gender unicorn came to save us, it would be amazing. People, everyone, would be freer."

I ask, "Can you tell me more? What would people be freer to do? And what would they be freer from?"

Mic raises their eyebrows and crosses their legs under themself on the loveseat, as if settling in before telling a story. "Well, to begin with, freer from all the stuff that goes with being either a boy or a girl, and then the assumptions of how to be either of those. And I think freer to do things, too, like what kinds of activities they like, or clothes and hair. And people will be free to not be mean and bully people about gender or who they like, because it wouldn't be a thing to bully people about anymore. I wouldn't have to worry about who I am and what people will think. I'd be freer to be a better friend."

Queering Your Therapy Practice is a book about having a therapy practice that, like Mic, is at once practical, full of wonder, and attentive to people's lived experience, yet ready to take flight into the imaginary. This is a practice that attends to the pain of injustice, while envisioning futures that are just and hope-full. It acknowledges the effects of sexual and gender-based oppression and violence. It supports courageous acts of resistance. It conjures a kind of magic in its capacity to create new and previously unimagined possibilities.

I use "magic" as Steve deShazer (1994) did when he borrowed Freud's words (1959) for the title of his book *Words Were Originally Magic*. This is the "magic" that constructs identities and creates worlds of possibilities through purpose-full conversations. It's the magic that led Mic and me to conjure visions of a Queertopia, a place where—with or without unicorns—Mic wouldn't need to endlessly explain themself. Instead, they would be free to be the kind of friend they want to be. This is the magic of language: *Abacadabra*, a word of Aramaic origin, translates to "I will create as I speak." Indeed, language, as a social practice, holds the power to make worlds.

Narrative therapy creates conversational pathways to possibilities. Earnest curiosity and the art of creative, critical questioning provide alternative routes to life-saving identities for queer and trans people as they find their way through the ever-shifting world of gender and sexuality. To support people on their journey through this emergent identity-scape, narrative therapy needs a conceptual compass—one that accounts for and reflects the lived experiences of people who take up sexual and gender identities that never point straight north.

I knew that, as a therapist, I needed a new compass. In the early 2000s, queer and trans people (particularly youth and young adults) started showing up in my practice more than ever before. As an "out" lesbian with years of experience doing family therapy across multiple levels of care, I'd always had a fair number of LGB clients. But what was different was why people were seeking my services. Increasingly, people were describing experiences—and feelings—about who they were that they could not account for with the usual identity categories and the language available to them in our standard discourse.

Sometimes this meant that people wanted to reject identity categories based on gender and sexuality altogether. These people often asked me, "Why should who I'm attracted to and have sex with require me to claim an identity?" They rejected the notion that who you *do* (or want to do) determines who you *are*. Sometimes it meant that people's confidence in the stability of their identity began to waver; they experienced a flexibility or fluidity in their perception of who they *were*. Their sexual interests and their sense of gender also fluctuated, in an experience of almost-constant liminality. What's the category—or the language—that we use for that?

Sometimes, it meant that people couldn't find an identity category that fit them at all. They identified with no language, no models, no stories of others who came before them. Or, if they found a category, it came in a stigmatizing and lonely world of otherness.

To transgender and nonbinary people, not seeing or hearing themselves reflected—or accounted for—in our language practices[3] meant that their legitimacy was suspect.

Often I share with people one of my favorite Wittgenstein quotes, whose resonance and pertinence can hardly be overstated: "*The limits of my language mean the limits of my world*" (Wittgenstein, 1953).

The words associated with sexuality, gender, and identity are constantly changing and emerging. Iantaffi and Barker (2018) point to "an explosion of words" relating to gender alone. People and communities create words to include—and make visible—ways of being in the world that had previously gone un-languaged (e.g., ACE, ARO, and nonbinary).

We also reject terminology that has medicalized origins or pathologizing implications (e.g., hermaphrodite, homosexual, and transsexual).

Also, the meanings of words can change over time. The meaning and use of the word *queer* has shifted several times over the last century or so (I address this in Chapter 1). The words we use are not only time contingent; they're also place contingent. That is, the terminology and phraseology used in one locale are not necessarily the same that are used in another.

So it's incredibly important to always check in with people about the language they use and the meanings they assign—even if you are part of their community, and especially if you're not.

One more thing: I almost included a glossary for this book, but realized that it's antithetical to everything I just said in the paragraphs above. So, rather than provide a list of definitions that will be, by the time of your reading, partly obsolete and partly incomplete, I encourage you to do your due diligence in checking in with each person you meet.

As I witnessed people's stories of becoming and their searches for belonging, I also heard their accounts of less-than-helpful and, too often, hurtful experiences with other therapists. My clients heard things like, "You have to be male or female. You can't be neither, both, or something else." Some were told that they were "in denial" if they resisted claiming a specific gender identity. When they told therapists of their own uncertainties, some therapists declared their identities for them ("You're gay, of course," etc.). They shared stories of humiliation and shame in which some of these therapists subtly, and some not-so-subtly, expressed their disgust with them.

When the mom of a 14-year-old trans youth told me that I was "the best therapist we've seen, because you don't have an *ish* reaction," I knew I needed more tools in my practice repertoire in order to provide the most meaningful and helpful service possible. Not denying the dignity and agency of people is a pretty low bar, but evidently some therapists were failing to clear it. I also knew that I was at risk of doing harm if I didn't cultivate understandings and practices that honored—and were responsive to—this terrain that people were traversing.

After that session with the mom and her child, I went searching for concepts and practices that would help me not merely avoid doing harm, but also increase the likelihood that I would "make a difference that makes a difference" (Bateson, 1972).

Queer Theory and Narrative Therapy Hook Up

Queer theory[4] (Butler, 1990, 1993; Duggan, 2002; Foucault, 1978; Halberstam, 1998; Rubin, 1984; Sedgewick, 1990, 1993; Warner, 1993, 1999) is a set of critical practices influenced by social construction, feminist theory, and post-structuralism. Queer theory focuses on questioning (through deconstruction) assumptions about identity; power relations; social norms and practices; and, in particular, gender, sexuality, and desire.

I found in queer theory not only the compass I needed to wander far off the beaten path of normativity, but also an ideal praxis ally for narrative therapy. Because the two share foundations in social construction and post-structuralism, and because they both reject the notions of interiority and an essential self, they go together like glitter and rainbows. Furthermore, both rely extensively on deconstruction (Derrida, 1967.)

Queer theory provided the ideas and language my practice needed, and narrative therapy put queer theory into action in meaningful ways. Since then, this alliance has been central not only to my conversations with clients, but also to a self-reflexive practice of entertaining doubt about my certainties.

These ideas are conceptual resources for me to draw on; they are not the stuff of my conversations. They are like apps I keep open in the back of my head, not the screen I share with people in conversation. Narrative therapy, especially, helps me co-create the conversational terrain I travel with clients, one that reflects people's lives, both lived and aspirational.

Queer theory and narrative therapy serve as a praxis that is indispensable in my work with people like Mic. I believe that you—and your clients—will find the combination to be an invaluable asset as well.

This book is for therapists who know they need to do *something* differently in their work with queer and trans people, even if they're not sure what that would be. It's also for therapists who have met some dialogical dead ends when in conversation with clients (or anyone) about gender, sexuality, relationships, and identity. And it's also for therapists who are familiar with queer theory, or who have found it to be personally meaningful, but who have not been sure how to put it to work in therapeutic conversations.

If you're a therapist who is competent in narrative therapy, this book offers a host of critical concepts and practical principles for integrating queer theory into your practice. It is likely that the ideas presented here will challenge you, at least a bit. I've found the stronger a normative discourse is in your worldview, the more you feel challenged. But don't worry, I'll provide you with plenty of ways to unpack and create some discursive space between you and those tenacious discourses.

If you are a practitioner new to narrative therapy, I present core tenets and practices of the approach so that you have helpful handholds as you read. The vignettes, transcripts, and reflexive questions will make narrative therapy visible to you, and you will see the praxis relationship shared by queer theory and narrative practice. Post-structural and queer theories are notoriously daunting in their density, so I do my best to make them both accessible and practical.

Queering Your Practice

This book is my invitation to you to queer your practice. Although queer is often used as an adjective ("he's a queer man") and a noun ("this event is for queers"), I suggest that using it as a verb is its queerest elaboration.

Queering is an ever-emergent process of becoming, one that is flexible and fluid in response to context, and in resistance to norms. When we queer something, we question and disrupt taken-for-granted practices and we can imagine new possibilities. Queering something breaks rules (usually discursive and social rules, and sometimes legal ones) in order to liberate people who have been held hostage by what the rules require or prevent.

What does this look like in therapeutic practice? Because queering your practice involves resisting, challenging, and operating outside of norms, it can manifest in many ways, including:

- Resisting conventional notions of professionalism
- De-privatizing practice and creating communities of care that connect clients to one another
- Positioning and consulting clients as experts in their lives, and in the things and events that affect them
- Rejecting notions of psychopathology and the medicalization of human experience

- Refusing to function as an agent of social control
- Talking about unicorns in therapy.

Each chapter of this book includes a case vignette that focuses on that chapter's theme or topic. These vignettes will include young people and adults. They will involve individual, relationship, and family therapy sessions. And they will show people addressing issues such as sexual orientation; transgender and nonbinary identities; sexual desire and practices; non-monogamous relationship structures; family rejection; suicidality; and parenting concerns. While my focus is on matters of gender and sexuality, I ground my practice (and I strongly encourage you to ground yours) in critical intersectionality. Thus, it's impossible for me not to consider the ways in which other systems of power and oppression operate in people's lives. To this end, I provide the social locations of the people in the vignettes I share, and I do my best to address issues that impact BIPOC[5] communities.

I've also provided Q-tips—practical principles and suggestions—in some of the chapters. Q-tips are pins to insert into your newly minted map of queer theory-informed narrative therapy. Use them as landmarks as you get your bearings. But don't get too used to them; as all things queer do, they're likely to change before you know it—and the terrain certainly will. And, as all family therapists know, the map is not the territory. Be ready and willing at all times to remove any pin and move it to a new location.

Chapter 1 provides the theoretical and philosophical foundations for the concepts and practices that I introduce throughout the book. It answers the question of not only what queer theory is but also what queer theory *does*. This chapter includes an introduction to social construction and post-structural theory, with emphases on discursive production, essentialism, and power relations. These hefty-sounding concepts are important in practice, and central to this chapter, which shows you how to use social construction and post-structural theory in practical, meaningful ways.

In Chapter 2, I focus on helping you listen for the normative discourses that shape your ideas about gender, sexuality, and identity. The chapter focuses on deconstructing these discourses and questioning your own assumptions about gender, sexuality, identity, and so much more. I also discuss intersectionality and the importance of understanding gender and sexuality in relationship to dominating discourses, such as capitalism, white supremacy, and others.

Chapter 3 introduces narrative therapy and highlights some of its fundamental concepts and practices, such as externalizing, double listening, reauthoring, and counter documents. I discuss the idea of praxis and the relationship between queer theory and narrative therapy, with an emphasis on reflexivity. If you're new(ish) to narrative therapy, this chapter will give you a solid foundation; if you're a narrative therapy vet, you'll find new ways to put your narrative skills to work in the application of queer theory.

In Chapter 4, I critique conventional practice ethics for, among other things, applying universal codes of conduct in a one-size-fits-all way. The chapter includes a special focus on the matter of multiple (or dual) relationships for queer and trans therapists working in their communities. This chapter looks at queering ethics as a way of being accountable, and of attending to power relations.

In Chapter 5, I critique two common narratives that therapists encounter when working with queer and trans people: the coming out narrative and the parental loss narrative. Through the vignettes in this chapter, I demonstrate some queer theory-informed approaches to coming out and to parental responses to their queer and trans children.

In Chapter 6, I challenge the notion that sex is an immutable, "natural" phenomenon. Instead, I situate sex (and the meanings we make of it) in discourse. I introduce Rubin's (1984) seminal work on sex positivity, and then pivot to the more current and nuanced notion of *sex critical* (Downing, 2012) practice. I discuss how a sex critical stance is ethically and philosophically in alignment with a queer theory-informed narrative practice.

Chapter 7 focuses on queer theory-informed narrative therapy practices for storying resistance to rejection, isolation, or violence. I discuss diagnosing discourses (instead of people)—and, in particular, the conventional narratives around suicide. Finally, I introduce response-based practice (Coates & Wade, 2007; Richardson, 2015), an approach that can be especially useful in working with the effects of violence and oppression.

Chapter 8 challenges therapists to approach ethical practice as seeing beyond the constraints of the therapist/client relationship, and working for societal change. I discuss transformational change (or, second-order change), audacious hope, dangerous ideas, and (with Mic) how to get to Queertopia.

The stories and vignettes I share are real; that is, they come from actual therapeutic conversations with real people who are grappling with real stuff. I have changed names and other details, and in some cases made composites of conversations that shared similar themes.

Abacadabra: Unicorns, Magic, and Transcendence

Unicorns have been associated with queer culture for some time. More recently, Trans Student Educational Resources created The Gender Unicorn in 2014 as a teaching graphic.

Unicorns are fun; queerness embodies a playfulness in its disregard of solemnity. Unicorns are queer in their otherness; they are not of this world. Unicorns are mythical, magical creatures, queer in their transcending of norms. The queerness of transcendence exists in its ushering in of ways of being and knowing that eclipse convention. For all these reasons, unicorns are fitting and familiar paragons of queer culture. And it was for all these reasons that I asked Mic about the gender unicorn. My intention was to bring out the magic-making of words—magic that Mic didn't know they could conjure, until I asked a question they'd never considered.

However, the potential for magic is not in the gender unicorn. Nor is it in any formulaic use of the concepts and practices in this book, or in a specific question that you can ostensibly use with all clients. You'll find the magic in the imaginations and aspirations of queer and trans people—people who live courageously and dangerously in resistance to the binding norms of mundanity. Your job is to clear a conversational path so that they can speak into being the worlds—the Queertopias— that allow them to embody their richest stories of their fullest lives. When that happens, you will know that the words have been magic, even if no one mentions a unicorn.

Notes

1. Mic uses *their* as a singular pronoun. Some people use they/theirs/them as singular pronouns when they do not identify as either (or solely) male or female.

2. Historically, GSA stood for Gay-Straight Alliance. More recently, some groups have changed their names to Gender and Sexuality Alliance. These are groups in schools that provide support for students through policy, political action, and social activities. GSA is now the widely used generic acronym, similar to calling the place where you exercise The Y.

3. In constructionist philosophy, "language practices" refers not only to literal words, but also to all social activities among people that involve meaning making, such as images, memes, relationships with the environment, non-verbal communication, and much that is "beyond words."

4. There are many elaborations of queer theory, some of which assert perspectives incompatible with other queer theories. To further complicate (or queer) the task of describing queer theory, some queer theorists insist that defining queer theory is itself antithetical to the project of queer theory: resisting definition and fixity.

5. BIPOC is the acronym for Black, Indigenous, and people of color. I use this acronym instead of POC (people of color) or POCI (people of color and Indigenous people) because it emphasizes the unique ways Black and Indigenous peoples relate to and are impacted by whiteness, while also remaining in solidarity with other peoples of color. For more information, see https://www.thebipocproject.org/.

1

WHAT IS QUEER THEORY?

All F'd Up

LaTrisha sighed and shook her head. "So, I come back to school after summer break, which was great, by the way—I had this amazing internship at the state Capitol. And some of the people on my floor in the dorm are like, 'Ohhh, we heard you're with that other R.A., Alexis. Does this mean you're a lesbian now? Or, bi?' I mean, god! I've been back on campus like a week and this shit is going on, and I'm supposed to be leading all the freshman orientation stuff. Give me a fucking break!"

I'd known LaTrisha, a 21-year-old cis Black woman, since she was a freshman in college. I provided her with counseling support throughout her father's struggle with cancer. Now she's an R.A. and a senior, and apparently dealing with other people's imposition of identity conclusions.

"Damn," I said. "That sounds super frustrating. What do you call it, the thing you need a break from?"

Without missing a beat, she said, "People's f'd up idea that we all gotta be a thing they can put their finger on…and keep it there!"

"Do you have any ideas about what gives people this f'd up idea?"

"I don't know. I mean, I get it; I guess I do it myself sometimes, too, but I try not to. It's like, we want to know who people are, or we think we know who they are, so we know where to put them in our mind. I suppose it comes from people always doing it."

"So, everyone does it and that keeps everyone doing it, is that right?"

"Yup."

"What about that is f'd up to you?" I asked. "What about that has you so mad?"

LaTrisha looked down, shook her head, and then looked up again and met my eyes. "I'm mad because I didn't think I had to make an announcement to date a girl. And, I certainly didn't think I had to get a whole new ID card stamped 'Q' on it. I mean, if I don't declare I'm queer or bi, people throw all this shade and say I'm homophobic or in denial. That's some bullshit! My favorite uncle is gay, and my best friend is queer. I was in the GSA in high school for three years. Why can't I just like who I want to like?"

"What ideas do you have about why people want you to declare a new identity?"

"Oh, you know... people assume they know who you are based on who you date or have sex with, so they want to put you in a place. It's all pretty dumb."

"Yeah, it's pretty dumb," I said. "So, do you see smart people making this dumb assumption?"

"Yup."

"Does that mean they're not so smart, or does that mean the assumption is really power-ful? What do you think?"

"Hell, yeah! The Force is strong in that assumption!"

"OK, General Organa! You said people 'put you in a place' based on who you have sex with. What's important to you about refusing to be put it a place, at least based on that?"

"So, I think it's about the assumptions. People assume straightness—that's the biggest assumption people always make, and it's f'd up. I never told anyone I was straight—they just assumed it, probably 'cuz I dated a dude for a few months. But I never said, 'Yo, I'm a straight girl!' But I totally think that assumption is part of what's happening now, because it's just like when people thought I was straight—I'm not supposed to change or be flexible at all. The assumption is that people have to stay the same. That's f'd up, too. Because that's what people want to put a finger on—what label they can pin on you! Now, they want me to choose a new label to fit their assumptions about who I am, now that I've dated a woman. It's all f'd up."

We both paused a moment. We let her words, and the revelations they carried, settle into us.

I asked LaTrisha if I could ask some more questions, and she agreed.

"For you, is the f'd up part that people want to label you? Or that they want you to stay and not move from a label? Or that they assume things about who you are, and don't ask you? Or is it something else?"

"All of it. It's f'd up that people want to put you in a box and label you; it's f'd up that they have assumptions about what those should be and don't ask you; it's f'd up that, once you've been labeled and sorted into a box, you're supposed to stay there; and it's super f'd up that people think they get to have an opinion about any of this. Why can't I just like who I want to like? Get with who I want to get with?"

When I share stories like LaTrisha's with other therapists, I often hear them say some of the same things that her friends told her: that she's in denial about her "true self" (i.e., her sexual orientation), or that she's struggling with "internalized homophobia." They hear her question, *Why can't I just like who I want to like?*, as avoidance of the inevitable: coming out to herself and then to others.

Conventional gay-affirmative practice would involve helping LaTrisha accept and love herself (not that there's anything wrong with that, but that's not what LaTrisha thinks her problem is) and to "claim" a gay, lesbian, bisexual, or queer identity.

But why? LaTrisha isn't hiding or minimizing the relationship she had with Alexis. In fact, she wants "to like who I want to and get with who I want to." She's contesting something else. LaTrisha is questioning identity categories based on sexual desires or practices. In a nutshell, this is also what queer theory does.

What's in a Word?

Before we address queer theory, it's important to talk about the word queer.[1] Until the late 19th century, people used *queer* as an adjective, and it meant "odd or eccentric." It wasn't necessarily pejorative or malicious; it was simply a way to describe a person or experience as peculiar.

It became a pointedly derogatory epithet, used as a slur against effeminate men and people with same-sex desires, in the late 19th and early 20th centuries. I grew up in the late 1960s and early 1970s playing "smear the queer." This was a "keep-away" game in which the person with the ball was "the queer," who was then chased and tackled by everyone else.

In the 1980s, in response to the Regan administration's deadly refusal to address the AIDS epidemic, and to an escalation of anti-gay violence, the radical activist groups Act Up and Queer Nation began using *queer* in their messaging. While the use of the word disturbed many (including some gay and lesbian people), it proved effective in disarming the word of its hurtful power.

This use of *queer* by queer people (against whom the word has been used) is an example of a *reverse discourse* (Foucault, 1978). A reverse discourse occurs when a group, instead of contesting or resisting a word or phrase that's used to oppress them, takes up the use of the word or phrase on their own terms and for their own purposes.

This taking back of the word *queer* has proven very successful. It has integrated into mainstream culture in TV shows like *Queer as Folk* (2000–2005); *Queer Eye for the Straight Guy* (2003–2007); and its 2018 reboot, *Queer Eye*. The mainstreaming of the word has led to its use as an umbrella term for all non-normative genders and sexualities.

Although this use of *queer* is ubiquitous, it is important to note that many people also use it in a disruptive and destabilizing way, one which intends to critique identities, rather than to establish or describe one. This radical and politicized use of *queer* is about challenging all forms of normativity and unhinging binary assumptions.

Queer theory organizes around this more radical elaboration of the word. Here is the definition of *queer* that I use in this book:

> Queer is a critique of identities, not an identity of its own; it stands in resistance to fixed identity categories; it stands against "normal"; and it signifies resistance to regimes of normativity.
>
> (Tilsen, 2013)

There can also be generational and regional differences in people's use of (and comfort with) the word *queer*.

What is the significance for you as a therapist of this fast and furious history of the word *queer*? Why do you need to know this history?

One important reason is so you can check yourself. Please ask yourself these questions:

- What do you think about the word *queer*?
- What are your reactions when you hear it? Is your reaction different when a straight or cisgender person uses it than when a gay or trans person does?
- Given your reactions, what might you need to do to be better prepared to work with people who prefer the word *queer* to describe themselves?

• What might you need to do to be better prepared to work with people who do *not* like the term, especially when applied to themselves?

In your therapy practice, if you typically use the word *queer* but your client doesn't, please don't call them queer. It is a very unqueer thing to insist that someone use the word *queer* if they describe themselves differently (Tilsen, 2013).

Now let's flip that around. If your client uses *queer*, use *queer* with them, even if it's not a term you would ordinarily use (or a term that usually makes you cringe). It's linguistic violence (Strong & Zeman, 2005) when we impose language on people that is different from what they use, especially when it has to do with their identity. Refusing to honor clients' language is a refusal to understand how language matters to them—and understanding is always our first imperative as therapists.

Here's another reason why this is important: when we understand that there are many ways people use *queer*, we are better prepared to suspend our assumptions—and, when someone uses the word, to ask them what they mean and why that meaning is important to them.

It can also further your understanding to ask someone who doesn't use *queer* why they *don't*—provided that you ask it to understand, not to challenge.

I always want to use the language that people use to describe themselves. I also want to understand what that language *does*, and how that's different from other potential ways of languaging their identities.

Lastly, it's important to be familiar with the history of the word *queer* because it illustrates the way power flows through language to produce meaning—and to create worlds. This is the process of social construction and discursive production. Narrative therapy is based on this understanding that language is productive.

As you continue to read, you will deepen your understanding of these processes and their relevance to your therapeutic practice.

What Is Queer Theory?

Feminist scholar Teresa de Lauretis (1991) introduced the term *queer theory* in her critique of the ways that gender, sexuality, and race—and the relationships among them—are conceptualized. While we can pin-point the coining of the term, the history of queer theory is a bit more complicated.

As with many complex ideas and methodologies, its origin is hard to identify because queer theory emerged from, and is influenced by, multiple critical traditions, community contexts, and practices. These include social construction; feminist theory; post-structural theory; lib-eratory and radical racial justice movements; the gay rights movement; AIDS activism; postcolonial theory; and queer, kink, and BDSM subcul-tures. Cultural influences and people's lived experiences have also shaped it. Indeed, queer theory emerged from the crucible of the academy, AIDS activism of the later 1980s/early 1990s, social justice movements, and the experiences of marginalized people.

Complicating all this is the fact that queer theory includes a variety of theories, many of which contradict each other. Thus, it's more accurate to say *queer theories*. Indeed, queer scholar Nikki Sullivan asserts that queer theory "is a discipline that refuses to be disciplined" (2003).

In my own practice, I integrate multiple concepts and methods from queer theory(ies) that work in concert with narrative therapy practice. I am not beholden to any one particular queer theory, and am willing to employ—depending on the client and the context—theories that contra-dict each other.

Queering Theory, or Theorizing Queer?

One simple way to define queer theory is as a set of critical practices that challenges assumptions about gender, sex, sexuality, anatomy, and identity, and the relationships among these. Queer theory includes the ideas of many scholars (e.g., Butler, 1990, 1993; Duggan, 2002; Foucault, 1978; Halberstam, 1998; Rubin, 1984; Sedgewick, 1990, 1993; and Warner, 1993, 1999) who work in many critical disciplines and fields of study. In particular, queer theory is indebted to feminist theory (especially Butler, 1990) for challenging naturalized accounts of gen-der, articulating how gender is a social construct, and exposing how power operates through and within gender discourses. In my work as a narrative therapist, the work of Foucault (1978) and Butler (1990) have been especially helpful, because of their emphasis on discourse and power relations.

Challenging binary constructions is a central project of queer theory. A binary assumes that there are only two opposing options available—for example, hot/cold, functional/dysfunctional, gay/straight, or male/female. Queer theory is especially (but not exclusively) interested in complicating the binaries around gender and sexuality. When we challenge binaries of any kind, we expose the assumptions that uphold them as culturally and historically contingent, rather than as ostensibly universal and "natural." When we deconstruct binaries that limit people's ways of being in the world, we open up possibilities for a proliferation of identities.

Queer theory is informed by social construction and post-structural theory. Thus, from a queer theory perspective, gender and sexuality are not inherent, natural qualities of people; they are social constructs that become institutionalized as cultural knowledge through the power of discourse.

This means that, depending on the time and place, gender and sexuality mean different things because of the cultural contexts in which they exist. Thus, gender and sexuality are culturally and historically contingent. That is, their meanings are dependent on how people interacting with them make meaning about them—and these meanings are influenced by their cultural and historical contexts.

Q-TIPS: QUEER THEORY

- Queer theory seeks to complicate prevailing assumptions about the continuities between anatomical sex, gender identity, sexual identity, sexual object choice, and sexual practice
- Queer theory questions biological theories of sexual and gender identity
- Queer theory questions the usefulness of sexual and gender categories
- Queer theory challenges binaries.

Let's take a closer at social construction and post-structural theory, and how queer theory puts these conceptual resources into action.

Social Construction: Constructing Worlds, Making Meaning

Before I discuss what social construction is, I want to talk about what it isn't: modernism and individualism.[2] You may not know it, but it's 99% likely that you are an expert in both modernism and individualism (which is a fundamental tenet of modernism), even if you're not very familiar with the terms or the concepts they represent.

Modernism is the worldview ushered in by the Enlightenment; it is the guiding framework that informs our understanding of social activities in Western culture. Central to this understanding is the focus on the individual. Modernism understands language to be descriptive and considers conversations to be social activities used to transmit or exchange information among people. From a modernist perspective, language describes truths. Thus, we often end up trying to prove that our truths are better than other people's truths.

Most approaches to therapy are situated within this modernist framework, which upholds individualism and considers therapeutic conversations to be about truths. This is important to acknowledge, because therapy is a conversational practice, and individualism leads to a particular way of talking.

Within individualism, conversations focus on what happens "inside" of people: inside their heads, inside their hearts, inside their "authentic selves." Thus, we focus efforts to effect change on people's *interiority*, that is, their "real" self that is somewhere inside of them.

We see this in most approaches to psychotherapy. These focus on changing thoughts or beliefs (inside your head), managing feelings (inside your heart), raising self-esteem (inside you somewhere), and being your authentic self (your "essence"). The idea of interiority is also related to *structuralism*, or the idea that inside of people are knowable, observable structures such as a personality and self-esteem.

Also central to individualism is *essentialism*—the notion that identity is natural and stable, and that all members of a particular group share specific fundamental attributes, regardless of culture or other contextual factors. One popular essentialist idea in North American culture is that all children and youth go through the same developmental stages (and that there *are* developmental stages for them to go through). Another is that men like sex more than women, and that women care more about relationships than men do.

Essentialism is a powerful and pervasive discourse,[3] one that is very easy to take for granted. But it is not the only way to view human interactions (though essentialism insists that it is). Indeed, as we will see, challenging essentialist ideas is central to queer theory.

In the story at the beginning of this chapter, LaTrisha ran into essentialism, as her friends struggled to make sense of her rejection of their efforts to fix a static identity on her, based on whom she was dating.

Why did I just spend so much ink (or so many pixels) and so much time describing what social construction isn't about? Because it's vital to recognize the taken-for-granted language practices of modernism, and to situate them within the philosophical and theoretical frameworks that inform them. This is also an important practice for understanding the ideas that we'll examine in the pages to come.

Also, by making modernism and its emphasis on individualism visible, we de-naturalize this dominant ideology. We see it *as* an ideology; we no longer take it for granted, or assume that it "just is."

This is an example of deconstructing dominant ideas and assumptions in order to avoid allowing them to go unquestioned, and thus (even if unintentionally) reinforcing them.

Deconstruction (Derrida, 1967, 1977) is a central practice of social construction and post-structuralism, and narrative therapists rely on it extensively. In the paragraphs you've just read, I've given you an example of what social construction looks like in action—by deconstructing what it isn't.

So then, what *is* social construction? Social construction[4] is a philosophical stance, or worldview, that stands in contrast to modernism and individualism. From a constructionist stance, we understand what language does in a completely different way than we do when we view it through a modernist lens. Instead of seeing language as *descriptive*, social construction views language as *productive*. That is, rather than communicating facts and truths about an assumed knowable reality, language produces—or constructs—meaning through social interactions. These meanings (and stories) circulate through discourse as people share and repeat them (Foucault, 1978). This is the process of social construction—or discursive production—in which people speak realities into being.

Q-TIPS: THE INVENTION OF HOMOSEXUALITY

In his seminal work *The History of Sexuality* (1978), Michel Foucault contends that the identity category of homosexuality is a modern invention, or, what we call a *social construct*. Acknowledging that all kinds of people have engaged in all kinds of sex with all kinds of people across time and place, Foucault points out that it wasn't until 1870, when Carl Westphal, a German psychiatrist, used the term *homosexual*[5] as a way of classifying people based on their sexual practices. Thus, an identity category was born. It's important to note that the term *heterosexuality* was invented at the same time, as the contingent against which homosexuality could be compared.

The idea of sexual orientation as an immutable, essential trait thus is very recent. Here is what Foucault said about this:

> We must not forget that the psychological, psychiatric, medical category of homosexuality was constituted from the moment it was characterized... Homosexuality appeared as one of the forms of sexuality when it was transposed from the practice of sodomy onto a kind of interior androgyny, a hermaphrodism of the soul; the homosexual was now a species.

(p. 43)

For your reflection: *How does understanding the history of the construction of these categories impact your thinking about sexual orientation and identity? What are the implications for your therapy practice?*

These realities are what Foucault (1978) called *discourses*—institutionalized ideas, and ways of talking about those ideas, that function as cultural meta-narratives.

Discourse has a regulating effect. We can never act outside of it; even resistance and transgression gain their meaning in relationship to the dominating discourses that they resist or transgress.

These ideas are central to a post-structural, or Foucauldian, analysis of power. Power is the ability to influence and shape social worlds through discourse. Queer theory focuses on exposing these power operations by deconstructing discourses—and the limitations they impose on people.

For an example, think back to LaTrisha's story at the beginning of the chapter. LaTrisha met head-on the power embedded within the dominating discourses about sexuality and identity. These discourses institutionalize the notion that one's sexual desires and practices constitute an identity (one's "sexual orientation"), and that this is an essential and static characteristic of that individual. Yet, as you just read above, this idea is very recent. Nevertheless, sexual orientation as an immutable quality inherent in all people is usually taken for granted in contemporary American culture. This is an example of discursive power. (Foucault would say that LaTrisha's resistance to it is also an act of discursive power, as it forms a counter discourse.)

Q-TIPS: COMPARING MODERNISM AND SOCIAL CONSTRUCTION

	Modernism	Social Construction
Truth	Truth exists independent of human awareness	There is no objective way to determine truth; multiple truths exist
Reality	Scientific reasoning, grand narratives, and objective reality	Ideological myths and stories
Culture	Objective, universal truths that transcend culture	Culture-bound knowledge; multiple truths
Language	Language is descriptive	Language is productive, and a part of power and knowledge
The Self	Identity is stable, essential, interior, singular, and independent of culture	Identity is ideological and culture-bound; a human being has multiple identities

The main shift from modernism to social construction involves a pivot from a focus on *objects or structures* (a visual metaphor) to an emphasis on *language practices* (a narrative metaphor). We shift from focusing on ostensibly observable "facts" to focusing on the stories people live—and we shift from talk about people's "true selves" to talk about their preferred identities.

Language does not merely *describe* a supposedly true thing that exists; language is the *action*—the interactive social process—that brings things into existence.[6] This means that we're interested in the process of constructing meaning (Bakhtin, 1981); what effects that meaning has; what it makes possible; and what it restricts. We're not just interested in what language describes. We're interested in what people do together (that's the "social" in social construction), and what that doing does (that's the "construction" part). In particular, we're interested in the effects of prevailing discourses on people's identities and lives.

Diving into Discourse: Stories within Stories

What are the implications of taking a constructionist stance in therapeutic practice?

Again, think back to LaTrisha's situation. Her frustration was a response to the way her friends understood what it means when someone is in a sexual or romantic relationship with a person of the same gender. From a constructionist stance, I viewed LaTrisha's understanding as evidence that sexual orientation is a construct. I also noted that her friends' reaction reflects the discursive power of this construct. I understood that the response from LaTrisha's friends represents a dominating, normative North American discourse—and that, according to this discourse, sexual orientation is an essential and natural quality or attribute everyone has (think Lady Gaga's *Born This Way*). I understood this, but I did *not* accept it as a universal, unquestionable Truth with a capital T. This allowed me to do several things including:

• Engage with curiosity about how LaTrisha made meaning of gender, sexuality, relationships, and identity
• Partner with LaTrisha in deconstructing prevailing discourses

- Consider multiple possible understandings, and their effects
- Situate her experience, the meaning she makes, and the meanings her friends made, in specific contexts, rather than as observable (and/or conflicting) truths

Thus, a constructionist stance positioned me to have a *generative* conversation—one that invited LaTrisha to expand on what she values and how she sees the world—rather than a *reductive* conversation, which would have focused on drilling down to the singular and universal "truth" of things. It allowed me to center our conversation on LaTrisha's meaning and on what mattered to her, rather than on imposing professional or cultural norms and values.

It also meant that I understood LaTrisha's individual story *in relationship to* the cultural stories in which her story is situated. This is a vitally important concept in social construction, and in a queer theory-informed narrative therapy practice.

This concept goes against a fundamental belief that is especially strong in the United States: the idea that we are the "authors of our own stories." This deeply ingrained platitude is both a product of American individualism (and essentialism), and a powerful means for perpetuating it. It's also both problematic and unconvincing.

Where individualism claims we have full authorship of our lives, and that we should "be ourselves," constructionism acknowledges that "we can never define ourselves outside of the prevailing discourses, beyond the boundaries of the culture's meta-narratives" (Tilsen, 2018, p. 19). We can never completely rise above, or move outside of, culture or discourse. Even when we embody identities or take up practices that *resist* dominating discourses, that very resistance is defined by, and in relationship to, those prevailing discourses.[7]

LaTrisha's experience demonstrates the challenge of trying to define oneself outside of discourse. It also shows that we're not the sole authors of our own stories. Our lives reflect stories within stories; that is, our personal narratives are situated within cultural discourses, whether we conform to the specifications of those discourses, or resist them, or do our best to ignore them. In this way, we are not the *sole* author of our stories, as we can never act outside of discourse.

Q-TIPS: SOCIAL CONSTRUCTION

Social Construction:

- Is a philosophical stance and worldview
- Maintains that truth is multiple, relational, and local
- Is not about observing structures (visual metaphor); it is about producing meaning (narrative metaphor)
- Questions "natural" accounts of subjectivity
- Rejects universal truth claims
- Recognizes that individual narratives are embedded within, and influenced by, discourse.

Power Up! (and Down, and All Around)

I've already introduced the ideas of discursive power and discursive production as central to a queer theory understanding of power. Now I want to highlight a few more key concepts from this post-structural view of power. It is important for you to have a working knowledge of these ideas, and of the main tenets of social construction (as discussed earlier), before we dive deeper.

As we've seen, *discursive power* refers to the ways in which, through language practices, power moves in the social world and exerts influence on people. (Remember: language practices include *all* social practices, not just those that involve words.) Foucault (1965, 1975, 1977, 1985) called power that moves through discourse *modern power*.

In Foucault's analysis of modern power, power is everywhere, and we are always engaged in power relations. Furthermore, Foucault maintains that the influence of power occurs simultaneously on the societal, cultural, and institutional levels, as well as on a smaller scale through personal interactions.

Because power is relational and contextual, it isn't inherently good or bad. It all depends on what effects that power has. Finally, power is always operating, and always moving in multiple directions.

Thus, unlike structural or liberal-humanist accounts of power, a post-structural approach does not view power as a commodity that some people have and others do not. Power is not a thing, but a fluid relation-ship. This means that, in all relationships at all times, we are engaged in power relations.

Let's pause and consider what this looks like in practice, by returning to LaTrisha's experience.

I understood LaTrisha's struggle as one born out of her grappling with the effects of the discursive power embedded within the prevailing ideas about identity, gender, and sexuality. She exercised power by question-ing and resisting these ideas as they occurred in discourse and in her relationships with her friends. (Remember, where there's power, there's resistance.) Here's some more from our conversation:

JULIE: What did you say or do when your friends asked you if this means if you're queer?

LATRISHA: I asked them why they didn't ask me if it meant I was straight when I was dating a dude last year.

JULIE: That's a great question! Was it important to you to not answer their question about being queer, or for you to ask the question you asked...or both?

LATRISHA: Hmmm....I think it was important to me to not go along with any of it. I just really think people can get with whoever, and it needs to be OK. And it's not the main way I think about who I am. So, I guess, all of it!

JULIE: What happened when you didn't go along with any of it?

LATRISHA: Well, there was some back-and-forth nonsense, you know, but I had some good conversations. Like, my queer friends, some of them totally get it, and we talked about how that's sort of the queerest thing, to not attach yourself to a label, and how that's hard because sometimes you do have to represent. I had some good talks with some straight friends—it blew their minds that it could even be a thing to not make sexual orientation a big deal.

JULIE: What's important to you about not making sexual orientation a big deal?

LATRISHA: Look, don't get me wrong. I want people who identify as queer or LGBT to be safe and have rights. I sure as hell don't want to be oppressed because I date women sometimes! I'm just not down with it being something people use to label people. It's just another kind of box to put people in. So, I guess it's important to me to fight boxes. I'm constantly put in boxes as a Black woman from a single-parent home, and being the first in my family to go to college. I've had enough of it. It's never for our own good. It's for the box-builders.

JULIE: You said that it's the queerest thing to do, to not take on a label. Would you say that by not doing the bidding of box-builders, you're queering social rules or expectations?

LATRISHA: One hundred percent! I'm all about queering the fuck out of things! Just set the box-builders spinning while we're out here doing our thing!

JULIE: What's your idea about who the box-builders are? Who has the authority to label people by whom they date? If it's not for your good, whose good is it for?

LATRISHA: Well... that all goes way back, right? I don't know who exactly the first box-builders were, but it's usually straight white men. (*Laughs*.) I can't even answer this without boxes! But that's definitely who benefits from the labels or boxes.

As you consider this exchange with LaTrisha, how would you describe her experience using the ideas presented in this chapter? What discourses did she resist? What constructionist and queer theory ideas do you recognize in my questions to her?

Through her skepticism, and her questioning of the prevailing discourses about sexual orientation, LaTrisha engaged in an act of resistance. This was itself an act of power in response to the power of discourse. In this way, she gained *author-ity*: the productive power embodied in one's "ability to write, speak, and live one's own experience from one's own perspective" (Tilsen, 2018, p. 31). Denborough (2014) calls this author-ity "story telling rights" over one's own story.

Because LaTrisha experienced the effects of very powerful discourses about sexuality and identity, her act of resistance and author-ity required that she construct a *counter discourse*—one that stands against prevailing discourses and gives meaning to a person's preferred story. For LaTrisha, this involved rejecting labels (and boxes) and queering norms.

Q-TIPS: QUEER THEORY'S INTERROGATION OF POWER

Queer theory investigates and exposes how power operates through discourse. It uses deconstruction to interrogate power, in order to make social norms visible.

Queer theorists ask:

Whom do these categories serve?
Whom do these categories include, and whom do they exclude?
Who has the power to define the categories?
How are the categories policed?
How do these categories change over time, and across cultures?

(Adapted from Doty, 1993)

Putting It All Together: Constructing Queer Theory

In order to introduce you to queer theory, I needed to spend quite a bit of time discussing social construction and post-structural theory. It's important that you have a grasp of these critical resources in order for queer theory to be legible—and usable—to you.

Social construction is a worldview, a philosophical stance. Within this philosophy are several theoretical traditions; queer theory is one of them. This is what I meant when I said earlier that queer theory is an elaboration of social construction.

Social construction and queer theory share several key tenets, including anti-essentialism; rejection of universal truths; focus on discourse; and interest in identity construction. I think of social construction as providing some of the foundational premises and methods that queer theory relies on. Queer theory provides the focus—gender, sex, sexuality, desire, relationships, identity, normativity—for putting social construction into therapeutic practice.

Think back to LaTrisha's story. LaTrisha's account is full of constructs such as gender and sexuality, as well as multiple categories (themselves constructions) within these constructs, such as men and women, and bisexual, gay, lesbian, and straight. Her story is also one of normative ideas about identity (it's static); sexuality[8] (it's an identity); relationships (who you *do* says who you *are*); and language (it's used to describe static, essential identities and beliefs that are universally understood). Because I listened through a queer theory filter, I heard these as problematic binaries and ideas imposed by the gender binary, heteronormativity, and homonormativity. Because I listened to her story from a constructionist stance, I heard cultural artifacts—ideas that are produced, shared, and perpetuated through discourse, which have very real effects on people. They certainly had very real effects on LaTrisha.

This is a critical point about social construction, one that people frequently miss. I often hear people say something like, "It's just a social construct—it's not real." Too often, they're pointing to something like race or gender. But here's the thing: social constructs have *very* real effects—not *despite* their being discursively produced, but precisely *because* of it. Societies have institutionalized entire systems of oppression around such constructs. These very systems point directly to the power of discursive production. Through language, we create worlds—all kinds of them—including those that marginalize, colonize, and kill.

This is how modern power operates. It does not require a central authority to enforce rules.

To varying degrees, depending on the privilege and position we hold in any context, we all enforce the operations of modern power, because we all participate in discourse. And, to varying degrees, we all participate in modern power by policing ourselves—by living up to the specifications of normative discourses.

In the next chapter, we'll take a closer look at these discourses—and at some ways to identify and question the power embedded within them.

Notes

1. I'm speaking here of the use of the word in the United States, where I live and grew up. Its history in some other countries is different.
2. Social construction is also called *post-modernism* by some folks, in some contexts.
3. Discourse is what gets to be said, who gets to say it, with what authority, and with what effects. Foucault (1970) defines discourse as a

"social practice" that circulates through culture and has a regulating effect on what can and cannot be spoken. Everything gains meaning through its relationship with discourse. According to Foucault, it's impossible to think, feel, speak, or act in a way that is free from its influence.

4.   It's important to distinguish *social construction* from *social constructivism*. Unfortunately, the two are frequently confused and used interchangeably. *Social constructivism* actually emphasizes the "in the head" process that people engage in individually to make meaning of their own perceptions. *Social construction,* the philosophy informing this book, focuses on the relational way people negotiate meanings *together* in the social world.

5.   An Austro-Hungarian journalist named Károly Mária Kertbeny coined the term *homosexual* in 1868 (Blank, 2012).

6.   I have tattooed on my arm in Hebrew letters the Aramaic word *abracadabra*. This translates to "I create as I speak" or, "with these words I create" and is a Kabbalistic (Jewish mysticism) reference to God speaking the world into being. I use it as a mnemonic for social construction or discursive production.

7.   Foucault (1978) notes the relationship between power and resistance this way: "Where there is power, there is resistance, and yet, or rather consequently, this resistance is never in a position of exteriority in relation to power" (pp. 95–96). In other words, resistance is always visible, and always has meaning, in relationship to power.

8.   The assumption that "sexuality" (meaning *both* one's appetite/lack of appetite for sensual pleasure *and* what we call sexual orientation) is something "real" that is knowable and universally understood is also a social construct.

2

UNPACKING NORMATIVE DISCOURSES

No More Role Playing

Dianne is a 48-year-old white, cisgender woman. She's also a single mom. She adopted Jackson, now 16 and also white, when he was an infant. They live in an outer-ring suburb, where Jackson is a junior in high school and Dianne is a nurse. Now they are sitting in my office, sharing the story of how they are facing what is, in Dianne's words, "their biggest challenge ever": Jackson's gender identity.

"I told her," Jackson said solemnly, "that I'm not a girl, I'm a boy, and that I want my name to be Jackson because I like the name and it starts with the same letter of the name mom gave me when she thought I was a girl." Dianne reached over and squeezed her son's hand as tears welled in her eyes.

Jackson was assigned female at birth (AFAB). Both mom and son described how he "never was a stereotypical feminine girl" and was a standout athlete, lettering in hockey and softball.

About four months before they came to see me, Jackson shared with his mom what he had figured out about himself after months of reading and watching other trans youths' personal testimonies online. This search, he explained, followed "years of thinking something's wrong with me and just pretending to be a girl as best I could. But I found out there isn't anything wrong with me—and that I'm not the only one who feels this way."

As we talked together, I learned how Jackson had an ah-ha! moment when he first heard a young person on YouTube describe themselves as transgender. I asked him, "What was it like before you knew the word transgender, and what did knowing that word make possible?"

Without pausing to think about it, Jackson said, "It made everything possible. Before I knew what transgender was, that it even was a thing, I thought something was wrong with me, because I didn't even know how to talk about how I felt. Now, I can talk about who I am and what's happening. And I have people to talk to about it who understand."

"What ideas do you have," I asked, "about why you had to do so much research to find the word? I mean, why do you think you'd never heard it before?"

Dianne smiled and said, "You know, we talked about that a lot, didn't we?" She turned to Jackson, acknowledging that it was his question to answer.

"Yeah, we did," Jackson said, "because I was mad that I had never heard it before and I had to spend months searching about it, and then reading trans people's stories online. I think it's hidden from people, especially kids, because some people think it's wrong."

"What might get some people to think it's wrong to be trans?" I asked.

Jackson thought for a moment before answering. "I think it's like a circle: if no one talks about it, it's like a secret. That gets people to think it's wrong, and then they make up stories about trans people, instead of actually talking to us."

I asked Jackson if I could ask his mom a question before getting back to him about what he had said. He agreed.

"Dianne," I said, "you told me that the two of you talked a lot about why Jackson had never heard the word transgender before."

"Yes, we did. We still do."

"Could you talk about how those conversations became so important?"

"Well, Jackson was angry, and some of that anger was toward me, because he felt I'd kept this from him. We talked about how I didn't keep it from him on purpose—it never came up because it just didn't occur to me that my child could be trans. I mean, I wasn't actively and intentionally not talking about it."

Jackson said, "So that's a whole thing, too, right? It's all part of it—no one thinks of it, like trans kids are invisible or not normal. That pisses me off!"

Dianne nodded. "Exactly, it makes me mad, too—yet I did it. So, we've talked about how some things people assume and take for granted, and not being trans is one of those things."

I asked Dianne, "When you were planning on becoming a parent, applying for an international adoption and all that goes with that, what kinds of things did you assume about your baby who you'd be taking home?"

Dianne nodded slowly and glanced at Jackson. "Oh, you know, the usual. I wondered if I'd have a boy or a girl. I didn't care which one. And I still don't. As long as he's happy." She smiled warmly at Jackson.

I asked if we could back up a bit so I could ask them about the anger they experienced, and they agreed.

"Jackson," I said, "your mom says you were angry at her. Why was that? Was there something that matters to you in your relationship that wasn't met?"

"Totally! She's my mom, so she's supposed to do what's best for me. I thought she'd deliberately kept this from me, so I was mad at her. Now I'm still pissed, but not at her,"

"What changed so that you're still pissed off, but not at your mom?"

Jackson thought for a moment. "Well, when I was mad at her, it's cuz I thought she kept this from me, and that's not OK. After we talked, I realized that, in a way, the possibility that I'm trans was kept from her, too! I mean, she knew that there are trans people, but, like I said before, it's not talked about like a normal thing."

"OK," I said. "I get that. So, what are you pissed off about now? Are you protesting or angry about something that's not fair—an injustice?"

"Yeah, I'm pissed off that our society thinks that gender is just male and female, and that how you're assigned at birth is who you have to be. That's what got my mom to not even think about my maybe being transgender. Now she's mad about it, too. So, I guess I'm protesting society!"

"That sounds like a big protest!" I said. "Jackson, are you saying that, instead of being mad at your mom, the two of you together are mad, and protesting society's ideas about gender?"

Jackson pumped his fist and said, "One hundred percent!" Dianne chuckled.

Over the course of a few sessions, Jackson and Dianne addressed a range of issues related to his transition. These included safety concerns at school; setting limits with Dianne's Christian fundamentalist family members; and making decisions about Jackson's participation in sports.[1]

One evening, Jackson asked to meet with me alone, without his mom. He and I had already been doing some individual sessions, so Dianne was fine with this. But in this session, Jackson was visibly frustrated as he sat silently on the loveseat across from me, fidgeting with a squishy ball.

I knew that he wanted his mom to schedule an appointment with the trans health clinic so that he could begin taking testosterone (T). I had already sent a letter of support to the clinic, and Jackson saw Dianne as "dragging her feet on T." For her part, Dianne consistently *expressed her support for Jackson starting T. But she also voiced her hope that he would "slow down and think about all the implications, especially for sports."*

Jackson's sullenness surprised me, so I asked him about it. He told me that he and Dianne had, in fact, met with the doctor. Jackson now had his prescription and had started taking T. Yet, he explained, he was "frustrated with my how mom is handling it."

I asked him to help me understand. Here's a brief segment from our conversation:

JACKSON: I feel like she's supporting me taking T, but she's not doing it happily.

JULIE: Are you saying that you'd like her to support you and do it with happiness? How would that make a difference for you?

JACKSON: It's like she doesn't really understand. If she really understood, she'd be happy to support me because she wants the best for me.

JULIE: If she really understood, then, she'd show up with happiness, is that it? (*Jackson nods yes.*) What do you think gets in the way of your mom really understanding and showing that she's happy to do what's best for you?

JACKSON: Losing her daughter. That's what it feels like for her.

JULIE: She feels a loss….What do you think it's like for a mom to do her best for her son, even if the mom feels it means she's losing her daughter?

JACKSON: It's really hard…and she wouldn't be happy about it.

JULIE: Jackson, it sounds like you have a lot of compassion for your mom. What would you want her to understand about how you experience her feeling that she's losing a daughter?

JACKSON: She's not losing a daughter. She never had one. I was in the role of daughter, but I never really was a daughter.

JULIE: When you were in that role, were you trying to believe it, too?

JACKSON: For sure, even though it wasn't the right role for me.

JULIE: What do you think played a part in your continuing to play that role? Do you think the things that had you play that role could be the same ones that have your mom feeling like she's losing a daughter? Do you think those things make it hard for her to understand?

JACKSON: Yes. We both thought I had to be a girl because of my body. She adopted a girl—what she thought was a girl. So, yeah, there's some of the same stuff, the assumption that your gender is what you're told you are.

JULIE: What is that stuff? What do you call it? I know we've talked before about social ideas and assumptions—is that what you mean?

JACKSON: Totally. Like the assumptions that there are only girls and only boys, and that it has to do with your body, and that there's something wrong with you if you transition. That has me feeling not like myself—even if I'm not playing a role anymore, and even after starting T. And it has my mom not understanding that I never was a daughter.

Acknowledging that social and cultural norms (such as the gender norms faced by Jackson and Dianne) impact identity is not a mind-blowing idea for therapists. What are often out of their reach, however, are concepts and practices that help bring these normative influences into the therapeutic conversation in ways that are accessible, meaningful, and useful to clients.

This chapter focuses on the normative discourses that are relevant when addressing matters of gender, sexuality, and identity. In it, I introduce deconstruction as a tool to examine discourses and their implications. I'll also introduce the analytic framework of intersectionality as a method for engaging with the complexity of multiple discourses.

Tuning in to Discourse: Listening to the World in the Room

The word discourse has more than one use and more than one meaning, so it's important that I be clear about exactly how I use it in this book.

Because queer theory and narrative therapy both draw on Foucault's work, in this book discourse refers to the cultural stories and meanings that are circulated through everything we do socially (Foucault, 1970). This includes when we talk to people; when we engage in social media; when we write and publish (formally or informally); when we share memes; and when we amplify some ideas and ignore, erase, or vilify others.

Prevailing or dominating discourses are meta-narratives that have great influence in shaping our assumptions, values, and beliefs. We may not be aware of them because they're so ingrained in our lives. We usually take them for granted and see them as "natural," rather than as the cultural productions that they are.

In Chapter 1, I noted that our personal narratives exist within, and are influenced by, multiple discourses. This is what I call "stories within stories," and it's at the heart of Foucault's assertion that we can't live outside of discourse. Remember, discourse has a regulating effect on what may—or may not—be spoken. Remember, too, that when we view language as productive, what can be said is not merely a matter of "free speech"; it's also about what realities can become possible in the world.

For example, think back to the account of Jackson and Dianne. Jackson initially described how he had struggled and suffered because he had never heard the word transgender. His lived experience—feeling like a boy, but being told he was a girl—wasn't reflected in the prevailing discourses of gender and identity that were available to him. This is an experience that I hear from many trans and nonbinary people. They feel adrift, and are often in significant distress, until they encounter the language that helps them speak themselves into the world.

In this way, discourse has everything to do with what gets to be an identity. As we've seen, not all stories are available to everyone at all times.

To be clear, in the example of Jackson, this is not merely a matter of an individual young person who had a limited vocabulary; after all, there are plenty of 16-year-olds who do know the word transgender. Jackson's story illustrates the power of a prevailing discourse. Jackson had no trouble learning how boys and girls are expected to be masculine and feminine. This knowledge—the specifications and rules of masculinity and femininity—is repeatedly shared and circulated widely through the dominating discourse. But, for many years, Jackson heard next to nothing about being transgender.

This is what Butler (1990) refers to as gender performativity: the repetition of gender norms to meet an idealized notion of gender. This is how Jackson knew how to play the role of daughter, though he felt himself to be a son.

If dominating discourses regulate what stories and identities are available, then how do alternatives even become possible? How do realities that exist outside of the assumptions of normative cultural narratives come into being?

Q-TIPS: EXPOSING GENDER TRAINING

Think about how you first learned what it meant to be a girl/woman or boy/man.

1. How did you learn this? Who and what were your teachers?
2. How were the lessons enforced? What happened if someone didn't follow the rules of femininity or masculinity?
3. Were the consequences of breaking gender rules the same for people assigned male at birth as they were for people assigned female at birth?
4. How did the training change as you got older?
5. When did you first become aware of anyone who did not meet the expectations of *either* femininity or masculinity?

A *counter discourse* is a narrative that stands in resistance to dominating discourses. Counter discourses are acts of resistance.[2] They emerge when people construct and circulate alternative stories in response to the institutionalized normative discourses that regulate and limit ways of being in the world.

Let's consider an example:

You'll recall that Jackson spent months reading personal stories shared by other trans youth. As Jackson learned about the lives of trans youth—lives that existed in resistance to cultural gender norms—an alternative became available to him. Nevertheless, even after Jackson had the language of, and stories about, trans lives, he still had to struggle against normative ideas of gender and identity. Counter discourses don't erase the effects of prevailing discourses; they open up alternative pathways than run against the grain of prevailing discourses. In fact, we can only understand counter discourses in relationship to the dominating discourses that they oppose.

Deconstruction: What's in Words?

How do we work with discourses so that they become visible to clients, allowing them to consider their impact on their lives?

Deconstruction (Derrida, 1967, 1977) is an approach to understanding meaning that is central to both queer theory and narrative practice. Deconstruction decenters dominant ideas by asking questions about the assumptions embedded within them.

Decentering dominance is important because, when certain ideas are centered—that is, given positions of dominance, privilege, or normativity—other ideas get pushed to the margins. For example, Jackson's experience of not knowing the word *transgender*, and his desperate search to find language and representations that validated his identity, demonstrates what happens when some ideas and identities are marginalized: they become the Other.

When we deconstruct a word, idea, or discourse, we unpack the meanings in it. This reveals things we take for granted, yet are not always true across all times, places, and cultures. Put another way, they are not the only truth. Deconstruction dovetails with queer theory's skepticism toward essentialist ideas and truth claims (Tilsen, 2013) by asking questions about things we don't usually investigate, because we assume them to be true and natural. Through deconstruction, we expose the centrality of one idea, which then allows us to subvert it and make room for previously marginalized ideas—and, perhaps, entirely new ones.

Please reread the first five pages of this chapter again. Then ask yourself these questions:

- What are some of the assumptions or "truths" that were deconstructed in that conversation with Jackson, Dianne, and me?
- What questions did I ask that facilitated the deconstruction of these ideas?
- What answers did Jackson and Dianne come up with that exposed the assumptions that affected them?
- What became possible once these assumptions were exposed and decentered?

At this point, you may have begun to notice things that you have taken for granted in the past—things that you're now questioning. How did that happen? What questions are you asking yourself. Which "certainties" may be in flux for you right now?

As you can see, I'm asking questions to deconstruct your experience of learning about deconstruction.

Beyond Binaries

Queer theory is especially interested in challenging binaries. This is a central task of deconstruction.

A *binary* refers to two related ideas that are defined against each other. That is, each is defined by what it is not.

A characteristic of binaries, according to Derrida, is that one of the ideas has privilege (it's centered) while the other does not (it's marginalized).

Another important (and problematic) thing about binaries is that, with only two possibilities, binaries ignore complexities. Binaries insist that things are either/or rather than both/and. Let's check out some examples:

- Healthy/unhealthy
- Trustworthy/untrustworthy
- Mind/body
- Thinking/feeling
- Safe sex/unsafe sex
- Man/woman
- Cisgender/transgender
- Straight/gay.

Stop here for a moment. I'd like you to back over the above list of binary opposites. This time, though, for each binary, come up with some ways of describing things that are not either/or. For example, something may be healthy for some people, but not for others; or, it could be somewhat healthy or unhealthy, but not completely one or the other.

Starting now, also watch and listen for binaries that show up in your everyday encounters and thinking. Ask yourself what is privileged, what is marginalized, and what is rendered non-existent by the binaries that you notice.

Hearing Queerly: Listening for Normative Discourses

Now that you have an understanding of what discourses are, and how deconstruction is a resource to unpack them, let's move on to some of the specific discourses that are especially germane to matters of sex, sexuality, gender, and identity.

A variety of cultural meta-narratives shape and influence our identities and actions, whether we're aware of them or not. Narrative therapy differs from many other practices, in part, because it focuses on exposing discourses to "give people an opportunity to decide how they want to respond to them" (Freedman, 2012, p. 7). In this section, we'll look at what discourses shaped Jackson's understanding and prevented him from having an awareness that transgender "was even a thing." We'll also look at other discourses that a queer theory-informed narrative therapist needs to be cognizant of.

The Gender Binary

We are constantly inundated with cultural messages about gender such as: "boys don't cry," "that's a woman's job," "boys have a penis," "this is a boy's toy," "women give birth," "act like a lady," or "pink is for girls." What should be apparent from these messages is that (1) there are two distinct and opposite genders (and only two genders); (2) that these distinctions are determined by anatomy ("natural" or "biological" differences), as well as by cultural rules and roles; and (3) breaking these rules, or stepping out of the roles, has consequences. These messages reflect and produce the prevailing discourse of the gender binary.

The *gender binary* is the system that imposes and polices adherence to two genders. The system hides in plain sight in so many ways that it's almost impossible to catalog them all—yet it constructs and shapes our assumptions about gender. The gender binary is ubiquitous. It appears in the first question we typically ask pregnant people (a category that we assume means certain things); in the toys, clothing, and activities we associate with and endorse for members of each of the two binary genders; and in our judgment of (and responses to) particular behaviors and expressions of emotion.

The gender binary is inextricably tied to the discourse of patriarchy, which dictates ideas about "normal" masculinity and femininity, particularly in regard to social power, authority, and privilege. It's impossible to work responsibly with issues of sex, sexuality, and gender without situating our discussions within these discourses.

Gender Essentialism

The gender binary is related to ideas of *gender essentialism*, another assumption of patriarchal ideology. Gender essentialism asserts that differences between men and women (remember, according to gender essentialism, there are only two genders!) are innate and universal (i.e., the same across all times, places, and cultures); that they are due to biological, psychological, and genetic factors; and that they are therefore, "by nature," unchangeable. Gender essentialism is responsible for ideas such as *Men are inherently domineering and aggressive* and *Women are by nature emotional and reactive*.

Cisnormativity

Cisnormativity (Heinz, 2012) is another powerful discourse that is related to the gender binary and gender essentialism. Cisnormativity is the assumption that people are cisgender[3]—that is, whatever gender they were assigned at birth—and that this is, forevermore, their only legitimate and acceptable gender identity. Examples of cisnormativity include paperwork that offers only "male" and "female" as options; women's and men's bathrooms; assuming someone's gender based on appearances (which require us to impose normative ideas about gender based on our read of someone's gender); and drawing conclusions about gender based on primary and secondary sex characteristics.

Gender essentialism and cisnormativity rely on stereotypes constructed within the gender binary—and, at the same time, reinforce them. This is how discourse works.

Because of the pervasiveness of these discourses, Jackson knew how to "be in the role" of daughter. And, because of the gender binary and gender essentialism, he had a hard time finding language and other representations of his gender experience as a trans young person.

Heteronormativity

The gender binary serves as the backbone of other dominating discourses that influence gender, sexuality, sex, and relationships. One of the most pervasive of these discourses is *heteronormativity*. According to Michael Warner (1991), the queer theorist who coined this term, heteronormativity is a set of practices and institutions that legitimizes heterosexuality as the only "natural" and legitimate sexual orientation. When we ask a woman who her boyfriend or husband is, we are making a heteronormative assumption. When we joke about keeping a good-looking boy "away from the girls," we are acting on and reinforcing heteronormativity. When we tell young people that they can't know if they're gay, lesbian, bi, queer, pan, ACE, or ARO[4] because they're too young to make these decisions, we are imposing heteronormativity (and adultism!).

Think about it: Are straight youth ever told that they're too young to determine that they're heterosexual? Unless they are surrounded by adults who are making deliberate efforts to subvert essentialist ideas about gender and sexuality, the answer is no. We don't question young people when they're straight because being hetero is the normative default.

This isn't only true for youth. Indeed, plenty of queer adults have been told that they can't know they're queer if they haven't "tried" heterosexuality, as if it's an ice cream flavor. Normative discourses get their power by thriving inside the assumptions we unquestioningly pass along.

Consider this vignette. Ty and Patrick are both cis gay men in their early 30s. They are a committed couple; Patrick is white and Ty is Black. They sought therapy with me because they were struggling to find ways, in Ty's words, "to move forward with our marriage plans without alienating our families."

As they shared what was making trouble for them around the planning of their ceremony, I learned that the issue wasn't so much between them, but, as Ty said, "the ideas that our families are putting on us about getting married." Here's how the beginning of our conversation unfolded:

JULIE: Can you describe what ideas your families are putting on you?

TY: So, my mom wants a big throw-down with all the traditional kinds of stuff you see at a straight wedding, stuff like the format, how vows are done, all the typical components of a wedding. I think it's fair to say, for the most part, that this is true for Patrick's parents as well.

PATRICK: Yeah, totally. My dad really wants a pastor of some kind—any kind—to marry us. We're having a friend do it. I think my mom has resigned herself to the fact that we're not using a pastor of any kind, but my dad…not so much. (*Ty shakes his head, chuckles, and says, "Nope. Not happening."*)

JULIE: How are your folks' ideas are at odds with your ideas about your ceremony?

PATRICK: I'd say our ideas are not so traditional; they're more radical. Queerer. Like, we're not following the script (*Patrick makes air quotes*), and we're doing things that are personal and meaningful to us about the issues that matter to us. It's way more political.

TY: We debated whether we even wanted to get married, not because of our commitment to each other and the relationship, but because of the institution. We've tried to explain this to our parents, but they don't get that we can have a committed relationship and also not sanction the idea that the government or church is what makes our relationship valid. My mom actually questioned if we're (*air quotes*) "really serious" if we don't want to get married in (*more air quotes*) "the right way." She apologized, but it still pissed me off, and I don't get mad at my mom a lot. I respect her too much.

JULIE: Given your respect for your mom, what does being pissed off at her say about what matters to you? Has something that's really important to you been overlooked or minimized in some way?

TY: For sure. What matters is that she has always supported us every step of the way. She talks about us having a "long life together." But now that we have our own ideas about how to have that life, our relationship is suspect to her, because it doesn't line up with her straight assumptions that your relationship can only be legit if you put a ring on it in a church and sign a state marriage license. What matters to Patrick and me is that this ceremony says something about our relationship—and those traditional things ain't it. I mean, we're queer—we don't have to do any of that!

PATRICK: My parents haven't come out as explicitly as Ty's mom. They haven't said, "You must not be serious if you don't get married in a traditional, churchy way," but they for sure imply it. Stuff like, "Oh, we thought this was going to be the *official* ceremony" or, "Now that it's legal, wouldn't you want to show everyone that your relationship is just as legitimate as anyone's?" It's super dismissive.

You can hear the many heteronormative assumptions in this example. These include not only the functional aspects of traditional weddings that the parents saw as "normal," but also the very notion that relationships aren't legitimate unless they're sanctioned by the state and the church. Even when two men are getting married, the norms of hetero-sexuality can take over. This speaks to the power of the heteronormative discourse.

Homonormativity

A somewhat parallel normative discourse is homonormativity, a term coined by scholar Lisa Duggan (2002). Homonormativity mimics heteronorma-tivity in its embrace of the same assumptions and values that uphold heterosexual institutions—and, thus, our cultural institutions in general. Homonormative ideas or values are those held by LGBT people that don't challenge or critique the taken-for-granted practices of a heteronorma-tive society. Homonormativity thus lacks a queer ethic.

Q-TIPS: THAT'S SO HOMONORMATIVE!

Heteronormativity is a fairly familiar term, but *homonormativity* is not yet as widely known. Because it refers to deeply embedded cultural institutions and practices, it can be a hard concept to grasp.

Here are some examples of homonormative assumptions, con-trasted to a position that reflects a queer analysis and a queer ethic:

HOMONORMATIVITY

- Seeking to serve opening in the military
- Gentrifying historically BIPOC neighborhoods with gay-affirmative businesses
- Working to legalize same-sex marriage
- Buying products and services from companies that advertise at Pride
- Downplaying sex and physical pleasure; emphasizing love
- Cis men playing trans women in TV and film roles
- Insisting to straight people that "we're just like you"
- Focusing on single issues that reflect the normative ideas of "gay rights"
- Celebrating individual consumption and wealth
- Portraying queer culture in pop culture with (overwhelmingly) gay, able-bodied, cisgender, middle class, white people.

QUEER ETHIC AND ANALYSIS

- Working to dismantle military imperialism
- Investing in communities and building local wealth
- Working to eliminate governmental sanction of kinship structures; making benefits available to all people
- Challenging anti-labor, racist, homophobic, and/or anti-environment practices
- Promoting sex positivity
- Hiring trans women to play trans women on TV and film
- Insisting that people see, embrace, and value differences
- Taking an intersectional approach to issues of justice; creating solidarity across marginalized communities and issues
- Working for the collective good and equitable access to resources for all
- Offering a range of representations of queer identities and lived experiences.

To see how homonormativity shows up in the lives of people we consult with, let's look at a couple of examples.

First, think back to LaTrisha's story in Chapter 1. Her refusal to take on a label of gay, lesbian, bisexual, or queer challenges the homonormative assumption of compulsory coming out. (Chapter 5 discusses the coming out narrative in more detail.) These assumptions include the idea that whom we have sex with is an essential and static identity (and, remember, the invention of "sexual orientation" categories is quite recent); that not coming out is a sign of "internalized homophobia"; and that coming out is necessary for someone's well-being (if their essentialized sexual orientation is gay). Insistence on coming out and claiming an LGBT or queer identity also disregards many intersectional complexities, as well as issues of privilege and oppression. I'll address intersectionality in greater depth later in this chapter.

Second, let's consider the experience of Gracie, a white, 16-year-old high school junior who identifies as a queer, bisexual, cisgender girl. Gracie attends a majority-white suburban high school, where she is a member of the Gender and Sexuality Alliance (GSA).

Gracie shared with me that, every year, her GSA chooses a community project to volunteer and raise money for. Gracie had suggested that the group volunteer for a housing program in their district that helps low-income people stay in their homes. She explained that she had "been hearing a lot about how there is less and less affordable housing in our community, because people keep building McMansions and tearing down apartments." Gracie said that she knows that "there are kids at our school who are homeless, or could become homeless, and queer and trans kids are homeless more than other kids."[5]

When I asked Gracie what happened when she raised the idea with her GSA, she said,

> The other members liked the idea, but the advisor gave us a lecture about sticking to gay rights stuff. He said that GSA only does community projects that have to do with gay rights. I argued that housing is a queer issue, and talked about intersectionality and solidarity with all marginalized groups, but he doesn't get it.

How did Gracie come to understand housing as a "queer issue," while her GSA advisor didn't? Gracie explained that her debate team had been reading about gentrification and how the contemporary gay rights movement had "gotten narrower because of capitalism and neoliberalism." She learned that, historically, queer politics had been more intersectional and had taken a multi-faceted approach to social justice. But the modern gay-rights movement rejected that approach in favor of things that were less radical, in order to fit in and be seen as normal. (I was impressed with her analysis and understanding; I didn't cultivate that kind of knowledge until I was in my 40s!)

As for her advisor, Gracie said, "I'm more frustrated that he's not willing to listen to us about what we think than I am about his taking a more conservative position. I'll put up with that, but he needs to listen to students."

I asked Gracie, "Given how you've described your commitment to an intersectional and queer approach to social justice, what makes it possible for you to put up with his conservative position?"

Gracie said,

> He comes from a different place. For him, focusing on what he considers gay rights is really important for him. He's a white, cis man with a master's degree. Gay marriage was huge for him. So, I get

him; but I think it's his job to get us, to listen to us and what we think it means *now* to address queer issues. It's our group, not his.

Gracie's experience is another textbook example of homonormativity (and adultism!).

Not all of my clients have had Gracie's analytical strengths, but they don't need to.[6] It's our job to attend to discourses and invite clients into conversations. In these conversations, we can, together, consider the effects of discourses on them, as well as bring forward ways in which they might (or already) resist discursive constraints.

I think of queer theory as an app that is open and running in the back of my head. It's a resource that helps me host a conversation that is richly situated within the many discourses that impact people and their identities. I don't talk using these terms and concepts (unless a client is already using the language of queer theory and discourse). Instead, I have a dialogue with people using their own language and ideas.

It's in this shared and constantly emerging conversational space that, together, we illuminate the relationship between cultural stories and the personal narratives of people's lives. Once this relationship is visible, new and generative conversational pathways emerge, leading to courageous acts of resistance—and people imagining new identities to live into.

Stepping into Complexity: Multiple Discourses and Intersectionality

The identities and lived experiences of every person who sits across from us are impacted and shaped by multiple discourses. In North America, people typically come to therapy not only with gender and sexual identities, but also with identities that are constructed around race, ability, class, national origin, age, and cultural ethnicity (as well as innumerable discourses that emerge from these).[7] As with sexuality and gender, dominating discourses circulate and reinforce stories about race, class, ability, ethnicity, age, and national origin in ways that impact people's lives. People's sexual and gender identities are interconnected with all of their other identities and lived experiences. Because of this, it's incumbent upon us as therapists to pay attention to this landscape of multiplicity—and, especially, to the crossroads where various identities intersect and contextual nuances emerge.

In North America, nothing goes unmediated by capitalism, white supremacy, and patriarchy. We cannot escape the effects of these discourses, even when we're focused on sexuality and gender. In fact, I propose that we can't escape the effects of these discourses *especially* when exploring matters of gender and sexuality.

Capitalism, white supremacy, and patriarchy, in particular, play crucial roles in the construction of normative ideals and standards that mark some bodies as "normal" and some as "other." Meanwhile, an entire industry now exists around trans healthcare, making "gender identity… something that is, to a degree, bought and sold" (Travers, 2018, p. 179). Regardless of whom we're working with, we need to take care to avoid the mistake of treating gender and sexuality as independent from these discourses. (Unfortunately, this is what queer theory has historically been guilty of (Barnard, 1999).)

Q-TIPS: WHAT'S CAPITALISM GOT TO DO WITH THIS?

Perhaps you're thinking, *Hey, I'm a therapist. What's capitalism got to do with helping people?* As you'll see, for a queer theory-informed narrative therapist, pretty much everything.

In North America and much of the Western world, capitalism—and, in particular, *neoliberal capitalism*, or *neoliberalism*—has become more than an economic system. It's become a way of encountering and being in the world—and it shapes every assumption we make about ourselves and our lives.

Neoliberalism refers not only to a political and economic system in which private corporations control wealth and goods, but also to the way this system influences and shapes social discourses and people's identities (LaMarre, Smoliak, Cool, Kinavey, & Hardt, 2018).

Neoliberal capitalism goes hand-in-hand with individualism; they both over-emphasize personal independence and under-emphasize societal effects on people's lives. It defines people as consumers, who compete for the most things and the best deals. Inside this worldview, "freedom" no longer refers to inalienable rights, but to the right to choose from among a wide range of products and services (Fisher, 2009). Neoliberalism also defines people as workers who compete for jobs; as vendors or sub-contractors who participate in the precarious gig economy; or as resources or commodities who are managed, and often replaced, by offices with the title of *Human Resources*. (In an extreme version of neoliberalism, people working for the most successful company in the world are constantly surveilled, forced to pee in bottles, and sometimes pass out on warehouse floors from overwork and dehydration.) When we have problems, neoliberalism has trained us to question our personal choices and individual responsibility, rather than to examine possible social inequities and oppressive policies that may contribute to our difficulties (LaMarre et al., 2018). This is a central aspect of neoliberal discourse.

Neoliberalism has far-reaching impacts on people beyond direct economic effects, and this impact should matter to any therapist who wants to provide meaningful support and help. When it comes to mental health—and therapy in particular—neoliberalism has a significant influence on how we think, talk about, and act in response to our problems.

Cushman (1995) points out that mental illnesses "are not universal, they are local" (p. 7). As such, we need to look beyond one-size-fits-all explanations in order to understand what's behind problems in people's lives. Faulty cognitions, misfiring biochemical processes, and personal pathologies are common explanations of mental illness that bear the mark of neoliberal capitalism and individualism. Indeed, in the very act of collapsing problems onto individual people, we participate in the capitalist practice of burdening individuals and privatizing social problems (Fisher, 2009; Tilsen, 2018).

Psychotherapy's complicity in this privatization of social problems goes beyond how we understand problems. It also can largely determine how we intervene with them. We push pharmaceuticals to make individuals happier and less anxious in a depressing and stressful world. Meanwhile, "providers" deliver therapy in 55-minute billable hours, treating symptoms and patching people up so they can go back and produce (as workers) and spend (as consumers). We focus treatment on "self-improvement" that helps people overcome personal deficits rather than situate problems within limiting discourses and oppressive social systems.

Fisher (2009) and James (2008) document how the rise of neoliberalism has corresponded with an increase in mental health problems.

Given this surge of stress and distress, we should be asking questions about the conditions that lead to these problems. We can ask these questions in partnership with our clients as we unpack the discourses produced by and within capitalism. In fact, Lamarre et al. (2018) assert that all therapists need to understand and attend to the impact of neoliberalism on both the macro level (e.g., policies that impact people's lives) and the micro level (e.g., therapeutic interventions and individual decisions and acts).

For years, critical theory scholars of color have pointed out that sexuality and gender are racialized, and that race is gendered and sexualized (Anzaldúa, 1987, 1991; Ferguson, 2019; Gopinath, 2005; Mercer, 1994). This means that we make different meanings, and circulate different stories about sexuality and gender, when they involve white people than when they involve people of color and Indigenous people.

We can extend these differences beyond race to account for a variety of discourses and the identities they shape. People's experiences of gender and sexuality are different within different cultures and communities (Iantaffi & Barker, 2018). Failure to see these differences—or assuming that everyone experiences gender and sexuality in the same way—results in a "white-washing" of gender and sexuality (Anzaldúa, 1987, 1991; Barnard, 1999; Moraga, 1996; Namaste, 1996). This white-washing imposes Western ideals, values, and practices as a default "normal" setting.

Q-TIPS: MARKING POWER: MAKING ASSUMPTIONS VISIBLE

You'll recall from Chapter 1 that power moves through discourse. Discursive, or modern, power refers to the influence that any given discourse has on the construction of norms and practices. This influence circulates through everyday social practices.

One way to track how power operates discursively is to notice what goes *unmarked* by language because it is the assumed "normal" or default position. (No need to say anything when we can just assume!) For example, if I say, "I have a really good doctor," chances are good that, in your mind's eye, my doctor is a white man.

On the other hand, we tend to specify, or mark, non-whiteness, femaleness, and other subordinate positions. Sports teams are a good example: typically, we speak of the US National soccer team and the US National *women's* soccer team, while on the collegiate level we have, for example, the *Tennessee Volunteers* and the *Lady Volunteers*.

In clinical settings, I frequently hear therapists in consultation name the race of clients only when they're not white, the sexual orientation of clients only when they're not straight, the religion of clients only when they're not Christian, and the physical ability of clients only when they're not physically fully able.

To be sure, making marginalized people and their identities visible is important; the problem lies in that we (mostly) continue to *only* mark marginalized positions, while allowing the "default" positions to go unnamed.

Try this: during the next few days, in casual conversations, make a point of saying:

- "White" when talking about white people, but not naming race when talking about people of color
- "Straight" when talking about straight people, but not naming sexuality when talking about lesbian, gay, bisexual, asexual, pansexual, ACE, ARO, or queer people
- "Able-bodied" when talking about able-bodied people, but not naming ability when talking about people with disabilities
- "Man/boy" or "male" when talking about men, but not naming gender when talking about women or girls
- "Cisgender" when talking about cisgender people, but not naming gender when talking about trans, nonbinary, or genderqueer people
- "Christian" when talking about people who are Christian, but not naming religion when talking about people who are Muslim, Jewish, atheist, Hindu, Wiccan, etc.
- "Non-immigrant" when talking about people who are non-indigenous and were born into citizenship, but not naming citizenship status or nation of origin when talking about immigrants and refugees.

Then reflect on your experiences. What was it like to do this? How did you feel? How did people respond? How were your conversations impacted by doing this?

Then ask yourself this: How do your own social locations influence what you do and don't mark?

In your therapy practice, be sure to acknowledge (by naming them) both dominant *and* marginalized identities.

More importantly, beyond naming, be sure to attend to how people's experiences are shaped by their social locations and the effects of systems of privilege and oppression.

So, how do you attend to the multiplicity of discourses and the relationships among the identities they shape?

I've used the term *intersectionality* quite a few times, but I haven't yet discussed its origin. The terms *intersectionality* and *intersectional feminism* were coined in 1989 by Kimberlé Crenshaw, a Black feminist legal scholar.[8] Crenshaw introduced the concept as an analytic framework for addressing the ways in which interrelated systems of power (in her work, white supremacy/racism and patriarchy/sexism) marginalized Black women who were involved with the criminal justice system. Crenshaw maintained that, because of the ways racism and sexism intersect, Black women experience oppression in ways that are distinct from what white women and Black men experience. Since then, this tool of analysis has expanded (e.g., Collins, 2009, 2015) to examine the ways in which people of various social locations experience oppression.

Intersectionality is not an additive model (Crenshaw, 1993; Sullivan, 2003); that is, an intersectional approach is not merely about adding up the various social locations one occupies (and thus determining one's positions of privilege and/or oppression). Rather, intersectionality examines the complexities that are created within the crucible of dominating discourses that produce systems of oppression, in which the whole is much more powerful than the sum of its parts (Iantaffi & Barker, 2018).[9]

Consider Cesar, a 27-year-old cisgender gay man from El Salvador. He is in the United States on a student visa while attending a doctoral program in environmental science. Initially, Cesar came to see me to help him "feel more confident doing public presentations in English, and make decisions about plans after graduation." One day in late November, he told me that he and his boyfriend Troy (a white American cisgender gay man he met at a queer student event on campus) had been arguing about Cesar's upcoming visit home to El Salvador over Christmas.

"Troy's upset that I'm not out to all of my family," Cesar explained. "He says this means that I've internalized homophobia—that I don't really accept myself, and, by extension, that I don't fully accept him and our relationship." Cesar explained that he'd tried to make Troy appreciate the realities for queer people in El Salvador. "I told him," Cesar said with tears in his eyes, "that I came here to the U.S. not just for school, but because I knew I would be safer to be myself here—and, hopefully, to find love. If I didn't accept myself, I wouldn't have done that." While Troy understood that it wasn't safe for Cesar to be fully out in El Salvador, he disagreed with Cesar about his need to maintain close ties with family members who were homophobic.

As we talked, Cesar shared that he loved his family and that maintaining his connection with them was non-negotiable. He found it shocking "how willing my white friends are to cut people off."

This was the thrust of the conflict between Cesar and Troy: Troy (and some of their mutual friends, all white) thought Cesar should cut off all family members who didn't accept him. Cesar acknowledged that he hoped for a day when he and other gay people in El Salvador would be accepted, but said that he would never consider turning his back on family. "It's not even a 'choice,'" Cesar said, making air quotes.

Using an intersectional lens, I understood Cesar to be caught in the crosshairs of a variety of discourses, all of which marginalized particular aspects of his identity and lived experience. On one hand, Cesar's identity as Latinx[10]—whose cultural emphasis is on valuing family connection—was under assault by dominating American discourses of individualism, homonormativity, and racism. On the other hand, he experienced oppression as a gay man in a traditionally (and colonially) Catholic country that vehemently upheld patriarchal and heteronormative values.

Let's look more closely at how these intersecting discourses impacted Cesar.

When Cesar's gay white American friends encouraged him to cut ties, they imposed the ultimate of American values: revering the individual over the collective. This is in direct opposition to El Salvadoran culture, which values the family over the individual. Uplifting the individual is also supported by the homonormative values of (1) compulsory coming out (which I will address in depth in Chapter 5) and (2) isolating and prioritizing a distinct gay identity over other identities. Furthermore, because homonormativity re-inscribes the values of white society, the imposition of this discourse on a Latinx man is inherently racist.

Cesar was also affected by the discourses of heteronormativity, patriarchy, and colonialism. These discourses engendered a significant degree of homophobia and upheld rigid assumptions of the gender binary, defining masculinity narrowly and in heterosexist terms. Yet, because of the discourse in El Salvadoran culture that values the centrality of family, Cesar found ways to live around the edges of these oppressive stories about gay men.

Living at the intersections of these multiple discourses generated complexities and contradictions for Cesar. As I listened intersectionally and attended to the multiple discourses, I was able to enter the complexity of Cesar's experience. I was able to understand Cesar as a proud gay Latinx man who was committed to his family in El Salvador, and who was also in love with another man. His gender and sexual identities were in relationship to a variety of different (and competing) discourses and systems of power.

Thinking intersectionally helped me avoid the trap of the single story, or the "right" story. I was able to partner with Cesar to hold many stories which he could move in and out of, depending on which discursive and relational context he was in at any given time.

It's a Discursive Life

Understanding the relationship between discourse and individual narratives is central to queer theory and narrative therapy.

Discourse is the landscape of queer theory-informed narrative practice; in order to navigate the terrain of people's lives and partner with them to map preferred pathways, we have to be able to see the discursive forest for the trees of individual people's stories.

In this chapter, I've highlighted some (but by no means all) of the discourses specific to matters of sexuality and gender. These are the discourses upon which queer theory targets much (but not all) of its analysis. What's most important is for you to cultivate your ability to tune into discourses and deconstruct their impact on people. This requires you to resist the constant pull toward normative practices that privatize social problems and perpetuate the burden of individualism.

And remember: each of the discourses I've outlined in this chapter is shaped by other discourses. Heteronormativity, for example, operates in particular ways in white people's lives—and it operates in some different ways in the lives of people of color and Indigenous people. Attending to these intersections is necessary for providing just and responsive therapy.

In the next chapter, we'll look more closely at narrative therapy. In particular, I will focus on the relationship between narrative therapy and queer theory, and on how narrative therapy puts queer theory into therapeutic action.

Notes

1. Student athletes who are transgender may be offered widely varying degrees of support, depending on the policies of each school and each sports league administration. For more about this issue, see https://www.transathlete.com/.

2. Foucault (1978) asserts that "where there is power, there is resistance (p. 95-6)." Here Foucault is addressing discursive power—that is, the power of discourse to produce, regulate, and limit social practices. Resistance is a response to the regulating and limiting effects of dominating discourses. Resistance creates alternative forms of being and doing in the world.

3. *Cisgender* is the term used for people who identify with the gender they were assigned at birth. This term is helpful for making visible the experience of gender for people who aren't trans. It also challenges our standard languaging practices of naming only marginalized identities.

4. The gay/straight binary is, like nearly all binaries, highly questionable. There are a variety of sexual orientations. Pansexuality refers to people who are sexually attracted to all genders. ACE is an acronym for asexual people—people who don't experience sexual attraction. ARO is an acronym for aromantic—people who don't experience romantic feelings for anyone.

5. A 2018 study reports that LGBT youth are more than twice as likely as straight, cisgender youth to experience homelessness, and that up to

40% of homeless youth are queer. For the full report, see http://voic-esofyouthcount.org/brief/LGBTQ-youth-homelessness/

6. Each model of therapy is informed by particular theories and uses a special language. As therapists, we shouldn't expect clients to know any of these concepts or speak the language of its approach. For exam-ple, a Bowenian therapist thinks and listens in terms of individuation and the multigenerational transmission process, while a CBT therapist tunes into core beliefs and automatic thoughts. We shouldn't expect our clients to have this kind of insider knowledge.

7. This is true for us as therapists as well, so it's equally as important that we reflect on our own relationships with these discourses.

8. Prior to Crenshaw's introduction of intersectionality, other queer and feminist scholars of color had written about ideas that, in retrospect, pointed to intersectionality—for example, Anzaldúa, 1987; hooks, 1984; and King, 1988.

9. For a more in-depth critique of the additive model, see Anzaldúa (1991).

10. *Latinx* is a gender-neutral alternative to *Latino* and *Latina*.

3

QUEER THEORY AND NARRATIVE THERAPY

Praxis Allies

I Can See Queerly Now, the Pain Is Gone

Lizzy, a white, queer, cisgender woman, and Em, a white, transmasculine individual met in graduate school 15 years ago. They sought therapy when they found themselves in unchartered territory as Em transitioned from the gender they were assigned at birth (female), to a more masculine-of-center identity.

The couple expressed concerns about how Em's unfolding gender identity impacted their relationship's visibility as queer. They acknowledged that Em's expression of a more masculinized gender rendered Lizzy's identity as a queer woman less visible to other people.

"Basically," Em explained, "we're worried about what it means for us when we 'pass' as a straight couple. In the eyes of others, Lizzy becomes a straight woman and we lose our queerness. We don't want that."

Lizzy said, "I'm committed to supporting Em's transition—it's consistent with everything I believe about people's right to self-define. I'm committed, but I'm struggling, and I hate that. I feel guilty that I don't always want to celebrate the things that are happening for Em. If I were not their partner, I'd be the one throwing parties for them."

I asked Lizzy, "What do you think is inhibiting your ability to celebrate as Em's partner the way you'd celebrate if you were their friend?"

Lizzy said, "There's something about being a partner—the kind of relationship that partnership is, and what gender means in it—that's the barrier to 100% celebration."

I asked, "How is being a friend different from being a partner in matters of gender?"

Lizzy explained that as a friend, she wouldn't have the same "investment in how the relationship exists and is perceived as a unit. People see a couple as its own thing. And the genders of the people in a couple make different kinds of couples."

"What kind of couple do you think people see you as?" I asked. "Is it different from how you want your relationship to be seen by others?"

Tearfully, Lizzy, said, "Yeah, that's just it. I know what kind of couple we are...but it's how other people see us that I'm getting messed up in. It's like I end up judging our relationship like they would."

"Sometimes," Em said, "I find myself trying to do something, act some way that shouts out, 'Hey, we're queer!' It's frustrating to get to this point in my life, to understand how I want to be in my gender, and there's still always, always, the reality that people are gonna see what they think they see, and not who you want them to see, not who you are."

Em voiced their understanding of Lizzy's struggle, and reiterated their concern about the effects of their transition on Lizzy, and on the relationship's visibility as queer.

I asked the couple what they would call this threat to their queer visibility. They talked with each other and, after a few moments, turned to me and said in unison, "Assumptions."

"Assumptions of the cis-het world," Lizzy added. Em nodded their agreement.

"Yeah," Em laughed. "Assumptions of Cis-Hets Everywhere: A.C.H.E., ache! It's a real pain in the ass!"

After we joked a bit about aches and pains, I asked the two of them if I could ask some questions about A.C.H.E. and its effects on the relationship. I was curious about how these assumptions operated—and on how Em and Lizzy pushed back, responded to, and resisted these assumptions.

Here are some of the questions I asked during our conversation:

- What are some of the specific assumptions of A.C.H.E.? What makes these so pervasive and powerful in people's lives?
- How does A.C.H.E. steal your relationship's queer visibility?
- Is there a handbook or style guide that explains what queer looks like, or what rules you should follow, so you can be visibly queer?
- Does A.C.H.E. have special ways of enforcing rules about how to be visibly queer? Does it punish you if you break these rules?
- While these are the assumptions of cis-hets everywhere, do queer and trans folks ever operate under these assumptions—or even enforce them? If so, how have you experienced this?

- *Have there been any cis-het people in your lives who saw your relationship as you want it to be seen—people who saw its queerness?*
- *When are you free, or freer, from the effects of A.C.H.E.? Who or what makes it possible for you to have an A.C.H.E.-free experience?*
- *Who do you each get to be when you're unencumbered by these assumptions? How does this change the queer visibility of your relationship?*
- *When these assumptions aren't erasing your relationship's queer visibility, what becomes possible?*

In response to my questions, Em and Lizzy said that they, too, had learned these assumptions very well—and that these assumptions sometimes took them away from being the partners they wanted to be for each other. They also noted how A.C.H.E. led both of them to doubt their own efforts to promote their relationship's queer visibility as much as they would have liked. Yet they both made those efforts to "live our queer identities through our values, politics, and activities."

I asked them, "How are you able to sustain and live into your queer identities—individually and relationally—despite a boot-camp level training in A.C.H.E.?"

Without missing a beat, they answered together, "Community." They explained that being with others who saw each of them as they wanted to be seen, and who validated their relationship's queerness, helped them resist the effects of A.C.H.E.

"Do you think," I asked, "that assumptions make the most trouble in your relationship when they get you alone, isolated from community?"

"Yeah, for sure," Em said.

Lizzy nodded her agreement. "I think A.C.H.E is very isolating and makes us forget not just who we are, but also that we're not alone."

"What ideas do you have about why A.C.H.E. causes more problems when you're isolated?" I asked. "And why is community an antidote to this isolation?"

Lizzy said, "I think we start to believe the assumptions despite what we know and value. When we aren't in a community that lives outside of cisness and challenges its assumptions, it's hard to hold on—it's like swimming against a super-strong current. You know, being in community is a queer thing to do—that's what's going to keep us queer, even if cis-het assumptions try to drown us."

Lizzy and Em's struggle to stay visibly queer after Em's transition is a common challenge for couples when one partner transitions. Addressing this concern in therapy, in a manner that honors both partners and their relationship, presents its own challenges. This is especially true when therapists get stuck in individualist conceptualizations of identity, and in problem formation that fails to account for the myriad ways in which prevailing discourses affect people's lives. The decontextualized trappings of individualism make it difficult to imagine a relational way forward that brings the partners together around a shared purpose, rather than focuses on each partner's own personal interests.

In this chapter, I will use my work with Em and Lizzy (along with some other brief examples) to introduce the key principles of queer theory-informed narrative therapy. This chapter also provides an overview of narrative therapy—and, in particular, of how this approach brings queer theory into therapeutic action. As you will see, queer theory is an apt conceptual ally to a narrative therapy practice.

What Is Narrative Therapy?: The (Slow) Elevator Speech

Let me begin this section with a loud and clear disclaimer: heaps of important and informative books and journal articles have been written about narrative therapy. My intention in this chapter is not to cover this rich therapeutic tradition in its full breadth or depth. Rather, I will focus on the key principles and practices of narrative therapy, and on the praxis relationship between queer theory and narrative practices. After reading this chapter, you should have an introductory understanding of narrative therapy, a clear idea about how this approach operationalizes queer theory, and an awareness of how queer theory can inform narrative practice.

So, what is narrative therapy?

Introduced by Michael White and David Epston (1990), and elaborated on by many others (e.g., Combs & Freedman, 2012; Denborough, 2014; Flaskas, McCarthy, & Sheehan, 2007; Freedman & Combs, 1996; Hedtke & Winslade, 2017; Madigan, 2011; Madsen, 2007; Nylund, 2000; Tilsen, 2018; and M. White, 2007), narrative therapy is based on the assumption that people organize and make meaning of their lives through stories, or narratives. Our life stories (and we each have multiple life stories) gain traction over time, just like stories in the news do—through circulation. When particular stories are repeated and shared, they attain a status of legitimacy, occupy the center of our page of life, and push other stories to the margins.

When problems occur, people can experience a *problem-saturated story* (White & Epston, 1990) that undermines and usurps other preferred stories. For example, Lizzy felt like she was a "bad partner" for not fully celebrating Em's transition. The story of her being a bad partner existed at the expense of other stories about her (including those that Em told about Lizzy being a good partner). Over time, this resulted in a *totalized* account, or single story of Lizzy. This account also collapsed the problem onto Lizzy's identity, ostensibly locating it inside of her.

Totalizing accounts typically rely on *thin descriptions*. A thinly described story creates little space for complexities, contradictions, context, and multiple meanings (Morgan, 2000). These stories often impose absolute truths, ignore power relations, and make use of professional language (rather than that of the clients). *Thick descriptions*, on the other hand, involve detailed, specific, contextualized accounts using the client's language. Thick descriptions lead to richer stories, stories that center people's intentions, motives, and meanings.

Narrative therapists collaborate with people to leverage their own skills and knowledges to bring forward, remember, reclaim, construct, and circulate their preferred stories. For example, Em and Lizzy's relationship had been captured by a story troubled by societal assumptions (specifically, those of heteronormativity and cisnormativity). Through the process of narrative therapy, they took back and elaborated on an alternative story—one that fit their values and aspirations—and then circulated that preferred story through their chosen community.

The process of narrative therapy is one of inquiry. Narrative therapists ask lots of questions. The purpose of these questions is *not* to collect information for a psychosocial history, or to render an expert opinion (e.g., make a diagnosis, formulate what the problem is and draw up a treatment plan, etc.). We do not ask questions that we think we have the answer to. Instead, narrative therapists intend the questions we ask to generate experience (Freedman & Combs, 1996) and new possibilities. We ask questions instead of making statements in order to center our clients' experience and authority in their own lives.

Think back to my conversation with Lizzy and Em. What kinds of responses do my questions invite? What did the questions make possible?

Notice that my questions didn't come out of nowhere, or from some predetermined place. Instead, they used some of the same language and ideas that Em and Lizzy used.

You'll recall that queer theory is an open app that's running in the back of my head, but what I share with clients isn't the code behind the app. In this vignette, that app helped me listen to discourses of heteronormativity and cisnormativity (among others), while using words that reflected Em's and Lizzy's experience. This allowed me to ask questions that made space for what anthropologist Clifford Geertz (1976) called *experience-near* descriptions. An experience-near conversation uses the words that people use to tell their own stories, and relies on the meanings and understandings that those people and their stories hold. In contrast, an experience-distant description imposes the professional language and meanings of the therapist onto the client (Tilsen, 2018).

A quick and useful checklist about narrative therapy involves a lot of what it is *not*—and what something *isn't* doesn't really tell us what it *is*. However, when we make a significant conceptual shift—a transformational, paradigmatic shift—such as the one from modernist therapeutic practices to narrative therapy, identifying what it *isn't* reveals the assumptions of the dominating discourses of therapy that we have come to take for granted.

Below you'll find several of the common misconceptions about narrative therapy—misconceptions that reveal much about the taken-for-granted assumptions of individualism, and the approaches to therapy that uphold it.

- **It's not "just telling stories":** Narrative therapy involves a deliberate process of inquiry. A narrative therapist engages in earnest curiosity, asking questions that deconstruct discourses, generate meaning making, bring forward people's struggles and their responses to these struggles, and invite people into the imaginary. This involves a *shift from monologue to dialogue*. In a monological conversation, the listener/therapist is the target of the speaker/client; in a dialogical conversation, the listener/therapist positions themselves as a co-narrator (Bavelas, Coates, & Johnson, 2000).

- **It is not reframing:** When I reframe something, I assume the position of sole author by asserting a new meaning. Narrative therapists aspire to assume a *de-centered and influential* (M. White, 2007) stance, one that honors clients' storytelling rights (Denborough, 2014). Narrative therapists use their conversational skills to shape conversations that allow people to make their own meaning, construct their own preferred realities, and leverage their own skills and knowledges.

- **It's not focused on, or influenced by, psychopathology or normative ideas of development and health:** In Chapter 1, I discussed social construction and post-structural theory as the philosophical and theoretical foundations of queer theory. The ideas from these schools of thought also inform narrative therapy. This may be the single most important and challenging distinction between narrative therapy and other psychotherapy approaches—those that rely on conventional Western ideas of psychological interiority and individualism, developmental models, one-size-fits-all notions of health and pathology, and de-politicized practices. Because narrative therapy emerged from philosophical, theoretical, and ethical traditions that differ significantly from modernist psychotherapy approaches, it's impossible to selectively pluck out some specific techniques, apply them like a coat of paint, and thereby successfully practice narrative therapy.

- **It is not "strengths-based" and does not "focus on the positive":** Narrative therapy is very interested in problems and the suffering they bring to people's lives. Narrative therapists do not avoid or minimize problems and a person's struggle with them. Indeed, narrative therapists take interest in people's rich accounts of problems and the ways they're in relationship with them. We're interested in the meaning people make of these difficult experiences. The skills and knowledges people have, as well as their responses to problems, have meaning in relationship to the challenges they face. "Strengths" creates a problematic binary with "weaknesses," as does "positive" with "negative." Binaries such as these ignore the context and complexities of many situations.

- **It is not focused on cognitions:** On the contrary, narrative therapy, because of its focus on language and discourse, is very much an anti-individualist, social-relational practice (Madigan, 2011). Language is a social practice, and meaning is made in the social world. You'll recall from Chapter 2 that personal stories have a relationship with cultural stories; this is the idea of stories within stories. People's narratives, situated within a larger discourse, carry thoughts, emotions, actions, values, aspirations, and visceral experiences that are beyond words.

As we move forward, you will see that a queer theory-informed narrative therapy practice is about exposing and destabilizing normative ideas in order to create space to imagine new possibilities.

Now let's take a look at narrative therapy's relationship with queer theory.

Queer Theory and Narrative Practice: A Praxis Relationship

First off, what is *praxis* and why is it important?

While the concept of praxis has its origins with the Greek philosopher Aristotle, it was the Brazilian liberatory educator Paulo Freire (1970) who brought it into the modern-day landscape of critical theories and practices. For Freire, praxis involved the integration of theory and application through self-reflexive practice. This integration is both relational (i.e., it involves dialogue and a relational ethic of accountability) and intentionally political (because it focuses on transforming the world). Praxis challenges the either/or tension between theory and practice. It calls on us to account for the implications of our theories and the impacts of our practices.

Reflective and *reflexive* are often confused and used interchangeably. But they refer to very different processes. *Reflection* is a process of thinking about an event, thing, or person without asking critical questions about our experience. In contrast, when we're *reflexive*, we consider critical questions about our experience by turning our attention back on ourselves and holding a mirror to our practice and the assumptions behind our experience.

In short, reflexivity moves beyond simply thinking about something. It is "an introspective process of examining what we do, what we know, and how we show up to the work" (Tilsen, 2018, p. 137). Certainly reflection can be a starting point for, or entryway into, reflexivity—but only if we let (or push) ourselves to go there.

Reflexivity requires both humility and intention. Engaging reflexively fosters praxis by cultivating a space for critical thinking and accountability, which, in turn, enhance the possibility of transformational change.

Q-TIPS: REFLECTION OR REFLEXIVE?

Questions we ask in **reflection** include: *What happened? What stood out for you? How did you feel and what did you think?* The focus is outward, on the event. For example, I might reflect on a session and think, *Those parents are frustrating—they don't seem concerned about their child's struggles. They talked a lot, but never asked questions. The kid is cool, though.*

Examples of **reflexive** questions include: *How would another therapist, from a different cultural background or with a different approach, experience this family? Why does frustration get in my way with these parents? What am I expecting of them? What am I failing to appreciate or understand? In what ways are my feelings and responses influenced by my race, class, culture, and gender?*

Focus on Discourse and Modern Power

Like queer theory, narrative therapy is informed by social construction and post-structural theory. Narrative practice also shares with queer theory a focus on discourse and its effects on people's lives. Queer theory and narrative therapy share an interest in how people construct their identities within discourse. In this way, both queer theory and narrative therapy "focus on contextualized meaning making, rather than on universal truths" (Combs & Freedman, 2012, p. 1036).

What discourses can you identify that were operating in the example of Em and Lizzy? Certainly, the gender binary is central to their story: Em's embodiment of a transgender identity is in direct resistance to the gender binary (and its sibling discourse, gender essentialism). The gender binary shaped the assumptions of A.C.H.E. More specifically, when people assume that the couple is straight, the discourses of cisnormativity and heteronormativity are in play. In addition, the discourse of homonormativity shapes ideas about what a queer couple "should" look like. In the couple's account, we can also see how individualism amplifies the effects of these through isolation: the privatizing of identities and romanticizing of couples took them out of community and made them more vulnerable to these prevailing discourses. As Lizzy pointed out, "Being in community is queer." That is, being in community creates resistance to hetero- and homonormative narratives of relationship and domesticity.

As you can see, these multiple discourses are not distinct threads dictating norms in separate facets of social life. Rather, they create an interwoven network of social systems and practices that reinforce cultural norms.

Queer theory, narrative therapy's post-structural underpinnings, and its focus on discourse all involve a particular analysis of power. (You'll recall from Chapter 1 Foucault's (1965, 1975, 1977, 1985) ideas about *modern power* and how this form of power flows through discourse.) By asking Lizzy and Em questions about the struggle they were experiencing, they were able to identify A.C.H.E., which describes the power of the prevailing discourses that impacted them. Lizzy spoke of judging herself based on normative ideas. Em shared that they, too, experienced this judgment, and wanted to resist it by doing something that "signals we're queer." These are examples of how, under the influence of modern power, we get recruited into comparing ourselves to social norms and policing our own behavior. These are two key features of modern power: self-judgment (or surveillance) and resistance. Notice how attending to discourse and power is a way of deprivatizing problems.

People Are Not Problems

Both queer theory and narrative therapy conceptualize a self that is non-essentialized—that is, identities are fluid and emergent, and shaped by context and discourse. Identities are "stories about ourselves" (Tilsen, 2018). This is a significant distinction from individualist and modernist notions of a fixed and stable self that is "inside of us." In therapy, this stance helps us avoid viewing people as inherently pathological or problematic. Instead, narrative therapists see people as being *in relationship* with problems, which are situated within and sustained by the power of dominating discourses (Combs & Freedman, 2012).

Narrative therapy's mantra is, "The person is not the problem, the problem is the problem" (White & Epston, 1990). It is through the practice of *externalization* that narrative therapists separate people from problems. This is a radical departure from conventional psychotherapy practice.

This difference makes a difference: problems—when not located inside of people—are part of historical, social, cultural, and political contexts. In the story of Em and Lizzy, for example, the couple named A.C.H.E. as the problem that was causing pain and difficulty for them. This problem did not exist inside either of them—or only inside their relationship.

Before they came to identify Assumptions of Cis-Hets Everywhere as the threat to their queer visibility, both Lizzy and Em took turns shouldering the blame for their relationship's troubles. Lizzy would fault herself for not being "strong enough to not care what others think." Em found themself "feeling selfish for putting our relationship and Lizzy through this." At times, they found themselves arguing with and blaming each other for the distress in the relationship. Having new language to talk about the problem shifted the conversation in three important ways.

Q-TIPS: SHIFTING FROM INTERNALIZED TO EXTERNALIZED CONVERSATIONS: PRACTICE 1

Let's have two conversations: first an internalized conversation, then an externalized one. Then let's compare what each kind of conversation invites.

Pick something about yourself—a feeling or quality you don't like, or that others have said is a problem. Make sure it's an adjective such as, *bossy*, *anxious*, or *insensitive*. Then ask yourself the following questions, replacing "X" with your feeling or quality.

1. How long have you been X?
2. What are you most X about?
3. Why do you think you're X?
4. How do you feel about being X?
5. What other problems come from being X?
6. Did you learn to be X from your family?

Now, take the same feeling or quality and change it from an adjective to a noun. For example, *bossy* becomes *bossiness*, *anxious* becomes *anxiousness*, and *insensitive* becomes *insensitivity*. In the questions below, insert your problem in noun form where there is a Y.

1. When did you notice Y making trouble for you?
2. Are there certain times or places where Y is more likely to show up?
3. What does Y get you to forget about yourself so it can make trouble?
4. Who does Y get you to be that you don't have to be when Y isn't pushing you around?
5. Why do you think Y feels like it gets to have its way with you?
6. When have you been able to put a stop to Y, or keep it from having as big an impact on your life?

(Adapted from Freedman & Combs, 1996)

What was the above process like for you? How would you describe the differences between the two conversations?

First, by identifying the assumptions as part of heteronormativity and cisnormativity,[1] Lizzy and Em were able to acknowledge how they acted in resistance to the assumptions that threatened their relationship. Instead of struggling with a deficit in themselves or their relationship, Lizzy and Em understood that the problems existed in the social world, not in (or between) them. Once they understood the problem in this new way, they were free to look for different kinds of solutions.

The second shift that resulted from locating the problem in discourse was freedom from the burden of guilt and self-doubt. Because they were no longer blaming themselves or looking for fault in each other or the relationship, Em and Lizzy could partner together to address the problem. A.C.H.E. was an identifiable and shared adversary. The couple was able to chip away at self-doubt as they understood that the challenges to the relationship came from the social world, not from personal inadequacies or failings.

Notice how externalizing de-privatizes problems and challenges the burden of individualism. Also notice how non-normative this externalizing is. As you'll see, externalizing is central to queering your practice.

Finally, situating the problem of A.C.H.E. in discourse gave Lizzy and Em space to craft a more nuanced understanding of how the assumptions threatened their relationship's queer visibility, and each of their queer identities. This space allowed Lizzy and Em to develop a richer understanding of what mattered the most to them and to their relationship. Together, they then articulated a shared mission and purpose for their relationship, and identified specific practices that helped them live into their desire to be visibly queer.

Thus, the narrative practice of externalizing is a practical way to manifest queer theory's focus on discourse and the disruption of individualism.

Q-TIPS: SHIFTING FROM INTERNALIZED TO EXTERNALIZED CONVERSATIONS: PRACTICE 2

In the column on the left, you'll see a statement that internalizes problems. On the right are responses that shift the problems from being internal to being located externally.

After reviewing these examples, write an internalized statement using your X from practice 1.

Then write a response to that statement, in which you externalize X in a question.

I've been really dysphoric, lately; it's getting really bad	*How is Dysphoria making things bad for you?*
I'm so anxious and worried that I can't get stuff done.	*What has Anxiousness and Worry convinced you of that keeps you from getting stuff done?*
I'm confused about how to support them.	*Has Confusion gotten you to forget what you know about how to support them?*

Before I move on, I want to address a common misconception about externalizing problems. I'm often asked, "Doesn't externalizing problems allow people to shirk responsibility, blame someone or something else, and let themselves off the hook?"

In fact, the opposite is more likely: externalizing problems invites people into taking *greater* responsibility than locating problems inside them does. Here's how:

When we externalize a problem, we position people in *relationship* with that problem. People can then consider what kind of relationship they want to have with any given problem. Do they like the effects of this problem? Why or why not? Do they want the problem to continue to have the same influence in their life? Externalizing invites people to take a stand in relationship to the problem, and to call upon their own preferences, values, hopes, and aspirations.

Externalizing allows us to identify not only the effects that a problem has on people, but the ways in which people can have an effect on that problem. This creates space for people to show up as someone other than who the problem says they are (Winslade, 2009). These spacious conversations make room for at least two different story lines: that of the problem, and that of the person or people in relationship to the problem.

This is central to a narrative approach: we are not committed to "discovering" and analyzing interior structures (e.g. "true selves" and what's "really going on" with someone); instead, we are interested in the stories people are living, who these stories allow them to be, and who those stories tell them not to be.

When we locate problems inside people, they have to struggle against something that's part of them. There can be a sense that they're stuck with the problem—that is, "It's just who I am." This conclusion reflects the modernist notion of the essential self. Locating problems inside people (whether in their genetics, their brain chemistry, their behavioral patterns, or their relationships) effectively *disinvites* people to take responsibility, and often leads to hopelessness. In contract, externalizing problems is a pathway to *responsibility through agency*. When we externalize problems, people can act on their own behalf in response to problems.

Externalizing is not merely a technical matter of linguistic gymnastics: *it is a practice informed by and reflective of the theoretical traditions that inform it.* Externalizing brings to life the concept of the non-essentialized self, a central feature of queer theory.

Consider Lizzy and Em: instead of being in conversation with people who were "bad partners," I was in conversation with people about the quality and kind of partnering they aspired to in their relationship. Consequently, they were able to partner with each other and take a stand against A.C.H.E., rather than grapple with some personal deficit within (or between) themselves.

Q-TIPS: EXTERNALIZING: IT'S NOT JUST FOR PROBLEMS

Therapists who are new to narrative practice often make the mistake of externalizing problems, while continuing to internalize what they consider positive qualities or strengths. This is a mistake for a few reasons. First of all, it's theoretically inconsistent and dishonest. We can't locate preferred characteristics inside people and see these as "natural," while locating problems outside of people and viewing them as contextual and discursively produced. In other words, we can't have our conceptual cake and eat it, too.

I'm less concerned about theoretical purity, however, than I am about engaging people in generative and meaningful conversations. This is the second reason to externalize skills, qualities, aspirations, values, etc., as well as problems. When we externalize, we put people *in relationship with* their skills and with preferred ways of acting and being. Externalizing conversations provides opportunities for having rich discussions about how certain attributes matter, the history of the attributes, who has contributed to them, and what people hope to do with them (Carey & Russel, 2002). It's also more generative than most other forms of therapy and inquiry. When we locate so-called strengths, positive qualities, and skills outside of people, they become flexible, fluid resources for standing up to problems and living into a preferred story. The same is true of values, hopes, aspirations, ethics, and intentions.

Now, please go back to the Q-Tips entitled "Shifting from Internalized to Externalized Conversations" on page 66. Do it again, but this time try it with some preferred qualities. For example, you might use *intelligent, compassionate,* or *creative.*

Confronting Neoliberalism's Effects on Identities

We've seen that narrative therapy focuses on the relationship between people's identities and the discourses they're situated within. Queer theory's project of examining neoliberalism is thus deeply relevant to narrative therapy. (Critiquing neoliberalism and its effects on identity has always been a central project of queer theory.)

Although there is little in the narrative therapy literature explicitly about neoliberalism, such a critique is also implicit to the practice of narrative therapy, for the reasons described in the previous chapter.

For example, the very notion of a non-essentialized, multi-storied identity rejects individualism, a foundation of neoliberalism. As we've seen, this anti-essentialism leads to the practice of externalizing, which resists individualism and privatization of social problems by locating problems in discourse. This runs directly counter to neoliberalism's decontextualized emphasis on personal choice and responsibility, as well as to its guiding myth of meritocracy.

Because of its focus on discourse and power, narrative therapy provides a process for examining the effects of neoliberal policies and practices in people's lives. In particular, the discourse of neoliberalism is adroit at selling the idea that people have psychopathologies that require them to purchase interventions on the market. These include everything from pharmaceuticals and psychotherapy to "self-care" packaged as third-wave coffee, spa days, and ordering take-out. It also includes the "selling" of narratives about who and what is normal and successful. Through queer theory-informed narrative therapy, people can free themselves from the trappings of neoliberalism, and generate and live into alternative stories that defy (and sometimes transgress) neoliberal norms.

Consider, for example, Kamran, a 23-year-old Persian-American queer cisgender man in his first job out of college. In one of our first sessions, he described weekly work meetings where the focus was "always the bottom line, which keeps getting moved—the more money this company makes, the more money they say we have to make." Kamran said that managers created competitions between teams "to go beyond our monthly required sales." The "winners" would receive $15 gift cards to Target. Kamran said, "I leave these meetings sick to my stomach, trying to figure out how to win a fucking gift card."

I asked Kamran about the stress he was experiencing; what work goals and expectations mattered to him; how he personally defined success; and what he wanted in and from his job.

Kamran said, "I don't have to pit myself against my co-workers to get something I don't need or want, and to do work that isn't required of me. It's insulting." He told me that refusing to participate in corporate exploitation was "a queer act of resistance, because that company doesn't need to make any more money off of me and my co-workers—and they need to pay us more, and not with gift cards."

Through our conversation, we exposed neoliberalism's insidiousness. In the process, Kamran also began to craft ways to defy (and sometimes transgress) some of his workplace norms.

Finally, queer theory and narrative therapy share an interest in de-privatizing people's experience in an isolating and alienating world. Queer theory challenges the disconnecting effects of neoliberalism; many narrative therapy practices foster connection, and question the individualist principle of going it alone.

For example, Em and Lizzy reclaimed their queer community by inviting others into their transition, and by cultivating opportunities for the queering of their relationship to be witnessed by meaningful and appreciative others. (I'll highlight some further de-privatizing practices in the pages that follow.)

In short, queer theory and narrative therapy share theoretical foundations that make them fitting praxis partners. In addition to providing a critical lens for the interrogation of issues of identity, sex, gender, and sexuality, queer theory also positions therapists to examine a wide range of normative discourses. Narrative therapy employs practices that put queer theory into therapeutic action. Together, they offer conceptual and practical resources for queering your practice by stepping onto conversational pathways that you may have previously not imagined.

Narrative Therapy: From Stories to Storying

Now let's look at a few more concepts and practices that are fundamental to narrative therapy. You'll recognize these concepts and practices throughout the vignettes and conversations in this book.

At the beginning of this chapter, I introduced the narrative therapy tenet that people organize and make meaning of their lives through stories. This is known as the *narrative metaphor*. When we work with this metaphor, we hear *stories*, not facts or truths (Combs & Freedman, 2012).

The problem stories people bring to therapy typically offer thin descriptions of people's lives and identities. When we practice narrative therapy, we understand that these are not the only stories available. In fact, a narrative therapist is most interested in partnering with people to generate *preferred* stories that allow them to live into their aspirations and preferred identities. This is a dynamic, relational process that reflects a shift: from passively listening to stories to actively and collaboratively *storying*.

Although it's beyond the scope of this book to cover the breadth of narrative therapy practices, let's examine a handful more closely.

The Queer Craft of Curiosity

Asking questions is the hallmark of narrative therapy, and questions are the conversational fertilizer of narrative practice. A good question feeds the conversation and allows it to grow in meaningful and productive ways.

Asking generative questions requires an earnest curiosity. Earnest curiosity requires us to abandon certainties and entertain what is possible. It also, at times, invites us to enter the imaginary.

This kind of question-asking is a queer craft; it goes against the professional grain of making statements, embodying certitude, and being expert. It requires us "to wonder beyond what we know…or think we know" (Tilsen, 2018, p. 90). The questions that drive a narrative therapy conversation expose and challenge normativity by encouraging people to wonder outside the bounds of prevailing discourses.

As you read (and reread) the vignettes and conversations in this book, I invite you to look closely at each of the questions I ask. Notice *what these questions do*. In particular, consider: *What kind of responses and conversations do the questions I ask invite? How do these questions facilitate a shift from stories to storying?*

Q-TIPS: THE THEORY BEHIND ALL THOSE QUESTIONS

Asking questions is a vital part of a queer theory-informed narrative therapy praxis. Unlike most statements, questions naturally encourage dialogue and partnership between the therapist and the client. This makes space for constructing new and multiple meanings (discursive production!). Questions center people's knowledges and ways of knowing, and they de-center normative discourses and expert opinions. Asking questions is central to deconstructing normative discourses.

When therapists ask earnestly and respectfully curious questions, they take a de-centered but influential position (M. White, 2007). This is a practice of accountability.

Think about it. Whose ideas are centered in a statement, and whose ideas are centered in a question?

Asking questions that invite a client's own ideas and knowledges also de-centers the therapist's "expert" power.

From Problem Stories to Preferred Stories

A narrative therapist listens for openings to a new story that doesn't fit the problem story, or isn't predicted by it. This is central to narrative practice. An opening to a preferred story is any kind of change, or new development, or new perspective, that differs from the way the problem story usually plays out.

The problem does not have to completely disappear or be solved in order for there to be an entry point to an alternative story. Exceptions to problems always exist, even when problems continue to make trouble.

For example, my client Lucas was a 32-year-old white gay cisgender man who was trying to rid party drugs from his life. He shared a story with me about partying one night. He said that he "purposely made plans to see my grandma the next day," because he knew that he wouldn't "go as hard and long." In other words, although the story of his use of party drugs continued, it changed in an important way. This new development—making plans "I knew I would keep"—made space to consider, encourage, and strengthen a new story of Lucas's ability to be in charge of his drug use—and to honor important relationships.

These plot twists can also be aspirational or imagined. Miles, for example, was a gender-creative eight-year-old who was teased at school because other students expected him to conform to normative gender specifications. The problem story had Miles convinced that he deserved to be teased because he was different.

Then, one day, while meeting with me, Miles drew a picture of himself "standing up to bullies." He told me that he was "imagining in my head that I tell them to stop teasing me." This created an opening for us to explore what mattered to Miles; how he saw himself as deserving of respect and kindness; and what was making it possible for him to imagine something different.

Other possible entry points to new stories include:

- **Inquiring about ways that people influence the problem.** In addition to asking about the trouble that problems cause in people's lives, narrative therapists ask people about the ways in which they have influenced (or can influence) the problem. For example, Sol and Aisha, who had a queer daughter, disagreed about how to support their daughter in encounters with extended family members who "are out-loud homophobic." These disagreements were causing problems for Sol and Aisha. I asked them, "Are there times that these disagreements aren't as big, or don't cause as much trouble? Has there been a time where you would've expected disagreements to make trouble, but the two of you found a way out of them?" These questions helped the couple see that the problem did not, as Aisha put it, "have us 100% of the time." This opened up room for an alternative story.

- **Asking about life experiences outside of the problem.** Sometimes it's helpful to ask when the problem isn't a problem. Izzy was a 17-year-old trans woman who was experiencing a great deal of distress from gender dysphoria (G.D.) as she prepared to travel abroad with her family. "The thought of going through airport security is bad enough," she said, "but then there's the whole dealing with people misgendering me in more than one language." I asked Izzy about times and places where she didn't experience G.D. Izzy looked to her own stories of "feeling so good about my gender" to help her remember "that I'm OK and I do have places I get to be me without G.D." As we talked, Izzy decided to create a list of stories of "feeling so good about my gender." This wasn't just a mental list. She wrote out some stories, and added photos, poems, and memes that Izzy and her friends created. All of these helped connect her to experiences where gender dysphoria didn't hurt her. From then on, she carried this collection of items with her when she traveled.

History of the Future

When we work with stories, we are interested in linking preferred stories from the past to those in the present, and on into the future. Connecting preferred stories in this way contributes to their thickening.

For example, Kit, a 24-year-old white queer nonbinary person, struggled with significant insecurity and self-doubt around meeting people. Over several months, however, Kit started to deliberately talk to people in social settings. Then they began attending social events, then volunteering for a cause, and eventually dating.

At that point I asked Kit, "Can you think back and identify earlier signs—things you did or impulses you had—that point to the steps you're taking now in connecting with other people?" This was a way to link Kit's present to their past. Then, to connect Kit's present to the future, I asked them, "Six months from now, what do you think you'll be doing that today doesn't seem possible—just like, six months ago, what you're doing today didn't seem possible?"

Multiple Perspectives

Asking about how important people in a client's life might view something often challenges a problem story's grip and provides a spark for alternative stories.

Take André and Marcus, for example. They were two Black queer cisgender men in their 30s who decided to open their relationship. At times, they struggled to identify the valuable skills and knowledges they had cultivated in their relationship that they could bring forward to help them navigate this transition.

Here are some of the questions I asked them to help them access these skills and knowledges:

> If you could see your relationship through the eyes of your best friends, what would you see that's hard to see through your own eyes? What would the people who know your relationship best say they admire and appreciate about it?

Introducing the perspectives of *meaningful and appreciative* others (as identified by your clients) helps people consider stories about themselves that weren't available to them from their own vantage point. It's important that these are the stories carried by *meaningful and appreciative* others, that is, people's whose perspective matters to your clients, and who hold your clients in high regard.

The Absent but Implicit

Each of us is always working with multiple stories. This includes not only the stories that people put words to—stories that are present and explicit—but also stories that are absent in words, but nevertheless implicit in the conversation.

This idea of the *absent but implicit* (White, 2000) is based on the work of Bateson (1979) and Derrida (1977). It suggests that we routinely make meaning of our experiences by comparing them to something else.

For example, if I say, "That was a really boring movie," I need to have some idea of "interesting" or "engaging" in order to understand "boring." Thus, in order to make sense of an experience, we have to distinguish it from what it is not—and, in order to talk about what is, we have to understand what it is not (Carey, Walther, & Russell, 2009).

Attending to the absent but implicit requires what White (2000) calls *double listening.* This listening involves tuning into not only the dominant, problem-saturated story that clients tell us, but also the unexpressed stories on the other side of those dominant stories.

How is this helpful in therapy? People's preferences, values, dreams, and aspirations are often embedded within what is absent but implicit. The absent but implicit points us to what matters to people—and, thus, provides openings to new and preferred stories.

For example, Keith, a 46-year-old straight, cisgender white man, struggled when his 16-year-old son Jeremy came out as queer. Keith told me that he felt "guilty for feeling bad about this. I want to support him, and I love him, but I'm not exactly happy about this. I feel like I'm not being a good dad."

I asked Keith, "What values do you hold about being a good dad that you feel like you're not living into?"

Instead of asking Keith about the guilt, I asked him about what exists *in contrast to* the guilt: his values and expectations about being a good dad. This opened a conversation about his values and vision for himself as Jeremy's dad.

Story Documents and Circulation

In therapy, constructing new stories that have lasting power requires more than generative and creative conversations. When new stories emerge in therapeutic conversations, it's important that we also offer clients documents that make these new and preferred stories available to them outside of therapy.

Narrative therapists often document emerging skills and knowledges, as well as other new developments that support preferred stories. We use letters, certificates, announcements, and other items as ways to extend the therapeutic conversation—and people's accomplishments—beyond the therapy hour. Sometimes these are called *counter documents*: documents that run counter to the problem story. They run counter to something else as well: in contrast to the conventional documentation practices of therapy, they highlight a client's achievements rather than their pathology. (You'll find several examples of these counter documents in the Appendix of this book.)

Some examples of documents that I use in my practice include:

- **Letters:** I send clients a letter between sessions with summary highlights and questions I thought about afterward. The focus of these letters is always on developing preferred stories.[2]
- **Gender euphoria letters**: When trans clients request a letter for medical interventions, I always offer them an alternative letter that documents their gender journey in their own words, on their own terms.
- **Awards and certificates:** I do this mostly with children. It's a fun and playful way to mark meaningful achievements and milestones.

While these documents can go a long way in furthering and thickening preferred stories, in order to really gain traction, preferred stories need to be circulated. Sharing documents with appreciative others, and folks in positions to support the preferred changes, keeps people up-to-date on new developments and stories in someone's life. Story circulation can also include determining whom someone wants to invite into their new and emerging preferred life. Narrative therapists always partner with clients to determine whom to share these stories with, and how to do so.

Lizzy and Em, for example, organized a gathering at their home with some of their closest friends and supporters. They shared with this group their need to stay visibly queer, and they told each of their friends specific things they could do to help support what they called their Queer Visibility Project. This idea emerged from our conversation in which Em and Lizzy said that "community" helped them sustain their queerness.

Other practices that narrative therapists use to circulate stories, connect people to community, and de-privatize therapy include:

- Outsider witness groups: people who witness and reflect on a therapeutic conversation
- Definitional ceremonies: events to mark important identity achievements
- Leagues or teams or posses of insiders (people facing the same problems), who connect in support of each other, either in person or virtually.

By now, I hope you've seen clearly how queer theory and narrative therapy are apt praxis allies. In addition to sharing key theoretical underpinnings, narrative practices bring queer theory to life in practical and meaningful ways.

For you as a therapist, praxis is also a practice of accountability. Through praxis, we ask ourselves important questions about what we do and what our doing *does*.

The repertoire of practices available to narrative therapists is both broad and deep. As with the mastery of any craft, it also requires a lifetime of deliberate practice.

Notes

1. Although Em had said "assumptions of cis-hets" (implying that the assumptions making trouble for their relationship were those held by cisgender heterosexual people), they went on to clarify that they were not blaming cis and heterosexual *people*. Rather, Em and Lizzy agreed that the assumptions came from dominant cultural ideas (i.e., discourses) about gender identity and expression, sexuality, bodies, and relationships. This clarification is important—and central to the

ethics of narrative practice. By locating the problem (in this case, the assumptions) in discourse, Em, Lizzy, and I were able to examine how cis and het people are also influenced—and troubled—by these cultural ideas, and thus avoid an individualistic attribution of the problem.

2.   For more on letter writing, see Bjoroy, Madigan, and Nylund (2015).

4

IS THAT UNETHICAL OR JUST QUEER?

An Ethical Stance for a Queered Practice

Not Just Any Rando

My phone rang. Caller ID told me that it was Andy—a friend, a well-known figure in the queer community, and a former co-worker of my partner. I answered the phone, fully expecting a community-related conversation. But Andy told me that he was calling on behalf of his 16-year-old daughter, Zoe. He wanted to know if I'd be willing to work with Zoe. He explained that she wanted to talk with an adult who was not one of her dads, preferably a woman.

I'd met Zoe several times at community events, and at smaller gatherings where my partner, I, Andy, and his partner Mario had all been invited. There were many overlapping circles of connection between my household and theirs.

Andy told me that Zoe "remembers that you didn't take any of her shit and made her laugh when she met you. She'd eat up most therapists. In fact, she did eat up a therapist a couple of years ago. She's really attuned to the world and gets pretty impatient with adults who don't get stuff."

"Of course, she does," I said. "She's 100% your kid."

Andy laughed. "Mario and I talked about asking you, and I wanted to see what you think. We're comfortable with navigating our relationships with you—this is for Zoe, not us. We really want someone we know will respect her and her politics, and who has a queered outlook on therapy. I mean, honestly, we feel much better working with someone inside our community than outside it. Zoe said she doesn't want to see 'just any rando,' so she's open to this. What do you think?"

"Well, thanks for thinking about me as a suitable adult-other-than-dads for Zoe. And, yes, I'm comfortable with figuring out how to navigate our relationships so that I'm responsible to Zoe, and to you and Mario. Let's first talk among us adults about how we would want to do that. Then we can figure out how to fold in Zoe and her thoughts."

Perhaps you raised your eyebrows when you read the previous paragraph. Many therapists would take a hard pass on the prospect of entering into any kind of multiple relationship (formerly referred to as a *dual relationship* in the professional literature) with clients.

A multiple relationship refers to any situation in which a therapist sometimes plays a role in a client's life in addition to that of therapist. This might involve being someone's therapist while also being in a book club together, or providing therapy for a young person while being in a professional or community relationship with their parents. Most training in professional ethics includes strong cautions against contact with, and connection to, clients outside of therapy sessions. This position assumes that, by avoiding multiple relationships, therapists are less inclined to exploit or otherwise harm clients, who may be vulnerable to their influence.

The professional codes of conduct of the AAMFT, APA, and NASW do not dismiss multiple relationships out of hand. Each of these professional bodies specifies that professionals are expected to avoid multiple relationships *where there is a risk of harm to the client and/or impairment of the therapist's judgment.* However, when we examine what is *not* said, we will discover a variety of potentially damaging assumptions.

In the box below, I've provided the statements on multiple relationships from each of these professional bodies. Implicit in these statements is the notion that multiple relationships are at best benign, and, more likely, potentially harmful. There is no mention of the possibility that such relationships could ever be preferred or beneficial.

Q-TIPS: PROFESSIONAL CODES OF CONDUCT

Here are the most recent codes pertaining to multiple relationships from the AAMFT (2015), APA (2003), and NASW (2017):

AAMFT: Marriage and family therapists are aware of their influential positions with respect to clients, and they avoid exploiting the trust and dependency of such persons. Therapists, therefore, make every effort to avoid conditions and multiple relationships with clients that could impair professional judgment or increase the risk of exploitation. Such relationships include, but are not limited to, business or close personal relationships with a client or the client's immediate family. When the risk of impairment or exploitation exists due to conditions or multiple roles, therapists document the appropriate precautions taken.

APA: A psychologist refrains from entering into a multiple relationship if the multiple relationship could reasonably be expected to impair the psychologist's objectivity, competence, or effectiveness in performing his or her functions as a psychologist, or otherwise risks exploitation or harm to the person with whom the professional relationship exists. Multiple relationships that would not reasonably be expected to cause impairment or risk exploitation or harm are not unethical.

NASW: Social workers should not engage in dual or multiple relationships with clients or former clients in which there is a risk of exploitation or potential harm to the client. In instances when dual or multiple relationships are unavoidable, social workers should take steps to protect clients and are responsible for setting clear, appropriate, and culturally sensitive boundaries.

In this chapter, I consider how queer(ed) understandings of relationships and community give rise to ethical positioning and practices that differ from those of conventional professional codes of conduct. This includes, but is not limited to, those concerning multiple relationships. I examine why working with queer and trans clients requires a rethinking of professional ethics. In addition, I introduce *relational responsibility*

(McNamee, 2009, 2015), the ethical stance that guides my own queer theory-informed narrative therapy work.

Untangling the Problem from the Problematic Solution

Let's begin by deconstructing the prohibition against multiple relationships—and making visible the assumptions that undergird this long-heeded cornerstone of ethical practice.

I want to be clear that there is no legitimate argument for allowing therapists to exploit their clients—not just sexually, but in any way that benefits the therapist and harms the client. The problem with the cautions against multiple relationships is in the *conflation of avoiding multiple relationships with avoiding exploitation and harm.*

In practice, unwise or unethical therapists routinely exploit or abuse some of their clients within the allegedly safe context of the very private professional therapeutic relationship. There is no evidence that avoiding multiple relationships actually keeps these therapists from abusing their power and positions. In fact, the opposite is true (Lazarus & Zur, 2002; Tomm, 1993; Zur, 2000a, 2000b, 2001): the greater the isolation, the greater the chance of an abuse of power.

Despite this evidence, the proscription against multiple relationships remains strong among therapists. This strength is due to the enduring influence of psychodynamic models of practice, and a focus on risk management (Lazarus & Zur, 2002), both of which favor a relatively distant and detached relationship with clients.

As you have surely intuited by now, neither risk management nor psychodynamic theories and practices reflect the principles of queer theory-informed narrative practice. The suppositions that multiple relationships are potentially harmful, and that therapists should avoid them, represent very normative attitudes and practices. There's nothing queer about them.

Indeed, as Everett, MacFarland, Reynolds, and Anderson (2013) note, assuming that therapists *can and should* avoid multiple relationships is a "privilege of some practitioners' distance from the lives of clients and normalizes this distance as a measure of professionalism" (p. 17).

Questioning what constitutes professional behavior is a very queer project, inasmuch as it's part of interrogating power operations and challenging normative ideas. For example, let's consider the assumed model of the professional therapist as distant and separate from the people who consult them. In practice, this is at odds with the reality of the relationships and communities that queer and trans people (and most other culturally specific and marginalized groups) create and participate in. Queer and trans relationships and communities are often web-like, with multiple points of connection and many intersecting links. Thus, from a queer ethics position, we might ask if it's ethical to participate in a person's emotional, relational, and spiritual life, and then retreat to a distant community.

Seen from this perspective, our professional codes delegitimize and make invisible the queer community's intentionally interwoven connections (Everett et al., 2013). They also pre-empt any conversation about the potential benefit of multiple relationships before it even begins. And they imply that no such benefit is possible.

Andy and Mario asked me to be Zoe's therapist because they know how and where I show up in community, as well as how I show up in relationship with young people. Having a queer therapist who is known to them through both social and professional networks felt, in Andy's words, "much more in line with our efforts to be relational, not transactional." Valuing relationship, community, and interconnectivity is a hallmark of many communities—as well as of basic human happiness. With marginalized communities, it's also often central to survival.

As a queer therapist working with queer and trans clients, multiple relationships aren't something that just *may* occur; they're a given. I can't avoid them. As a member of a statistically small and politically marginalized sub-population—and as someone who shows up regularly at community and social events—it's inevitable that I'll have some connections with some of the people who seek my services. (And I live in a large city. This overlap is even more unavoidable among queer therapists who live in rural areas and small towns.)

Compounding this is the simple matter of client choice: queer and trans people often seek queer and trans therapists (MacFarlane, 2003). It should be no surprise that queer and trans people may not want to talk about their personal lives with someone whose experiences differ greatly from their own—and who may also represent a group that they see as dominant or oppressive. This can be especially true for BIPOC queer and trans people. For BIPOC queer and trans therapists, the chances of having lives that intersect with those of their clients increase with the number of their intersecting identities and communities.

Furthermore, working with a therapist who is a member of one's own community, and who shares social locations and lived experiences, can be especially helpful and healing. This is particularly true when your identity has been weaponized against you—and when you have been blamed for the distress you experience. This separation of individuals from their communities and cultural homes is a long-standing tactic of colonial and capitalist systems of oppression. When we impose a universal ethic—one that reflects and maintains heteronormative values—we de-value and dismiss local understandings and relational practices.

MacFarlane (2003) interviewed queer, trans, and Two Spirit[1] people who indicated that they would prefer to see therapists who are themselves queer, trans, or Two Spirit—and with whom they already have some connections. As MacFarlane observes, for people who experience systemic and institutionalized marginalization, seeking and receiving therapeutic support from within their own community is both an act of resistance to oppression and a practice of healing and resilience.

Seen through a queer-informed lens, our current professional policies on multiple relationships actually serve to police queer and trans communities. They may also inhibit health and healing.

Navigating the Complexities: Structuring Accountability in Multiple Relationships

Unlike the universality of rules-based professional codes, queer relational ethics involve a dynamic, ongoing negotiation of relational arrangements, informed by an analysis of power. When we assume a queered ethical stance instead of a universalized rules-based ethics, we entertain a variety of alternative ways of being helpful to others—ways that center queer and trans people and their preferences.

This involves stepping into complexity and intentionally structuring the relationships we form with clients. It's especially important to address where there will and won't be overlap in the lives of queer and trans therapists and their clients. One example: there may be a specific community space (perhaps a bar, coffee shop, bookstore, performance space, or social media platform) which the client would prefer that the therapist not frequent. Another example: a therapist may feel that it's appropriate to attend their client's drag performance when invited, but not if they haven't been given an explicit invitation.

Accounting for power relations in multiple relationships, and anticipating potential dilemmas, is central to navigating the complexities involved. This means that therapists need to ask themselves (and, often, their potential and current clients) critical questions about the effects on the therapeutic alliance and outcomes. Therapists need to do this not only before entering into a therapeutic relationship, but also throughout that relationship.

In my work with Zoe, for example, Andy, Mario, and I discussed in advance where we'd be likely to encounter each other, both with and without Zoe (and both deliberately and by chance). Then we decided how we would interact with each other in each situation.

MacFarlane et al. (2010) suggest a set of relationship guidelines for navigating the complexities of multiple relationships. These guidelines, listed below, are organized around informed consent, transparency, and the mindful participation of each therapist, client, and supervisor/consultant:

- Anticipate and identify where a multiple relationship has existed or may exist, and any concerns or issues within each context
- Identify any potential harm and benefits to the client, the therapist, and/or related others
- Discuss any other potential impacts of the client's and therapist's participation in a shared community
- Identify ways to reduce potential harm
- Identify where each party wants privacy or wants to avoid contact
- Identify how client confidentiality will be maintained outside of the therapy room
- Facilitate informed consent by the client; work with the client to create a plan for handling all of the above. This should include the client's right to terminate the counseling relationship and to seek therapy with someone else
- Engage the supervisor/consultant in the process. This should include creating a plan for routine supervision, and a plan for what

to do in the event that the therapist can no longer uphold their client's best interests

- Articulate the therapist's responsibilities with client in and out of therapy settings
- Consider if terminating the therapeutic relationship and referring the client to another therapist is the best alternative
- Document the entire process, including consultations and any adaptations.

(adapted from MacFarlane et al., 2010)

The goal here is to create a clear and open process within which all parties can negotiate and navigate the complexities of their relationships. This not only more authentically avoids the potential for client exploitation; it also encourages a relational arrangement that may actually be beneficial.

Stepping into these complexities is a queer practice—one that helps us resist the heteronormative values reflected within the legalistic, one-size-fits-all stance against multiple relationships.

How practitioners approach the notion of "boundaries" (the issue at the center of multiple relationships) is very much influenced by their practice orientation. As Dietz and Thompson (2004) suggest, there is little question among professionals about the need for boundaries in our client relationships, but "how such limits are defined and who defines them" (p. 2) varies widely according to theoretical orientations and approaches to practice. Theoretical orientations, and the models of practice they inform, inevitably reflect particular cultural norms and values.

In therapy, for example, the conventional notion of "boundaries"—defined by Peterson (1992) as "the limits that allow for a safe connection based on the client's needs" (p. 74)—emerges from psychoanalytic traditions (e.g., "ego boundaries"). This tradition asserts that people achieve psychological wellness through separation and independence from others (Greenspan, 1995; Jordan, 1991, 1997). We can also see the influence of the medical model and the scientific method on our traditional ideas about boundaries. These frameworks position therapists as experts, and they maintain that relational distance is required for successful outcomes (Dietz & Thompson, 2004).

The distance prescribed between therapist and client also strongly reflects patriarchal norms of individualism and autonomy, as well as the paternalism inherent in an expert stance. This "distance model" (Greenspan, 1995) institutes "a hierarchical relationship between professional and client" (Dietz & Thompson, 2004, p. 9) that perpetuates patriarchal systems of oppression by exerting expert power over clients. Caring and relational engagement (which are core ethical principles of some communities and cultures) are feminized, de-valued, seen as inferior, and sometimes proscribed. Thus, conventional ethics treat multiple relationships as a "boundary violation"—but it is more accurate to say that it is a violation of norms shaped by Eurocentric and patriarchal values of separation, individualism, and the power of the expert.

Indeed, Everett et al. (2013) assert that demanding the avoidance of dual relationships invisibilizes and simplifies the social context and practices of queer and trans communities. Reynolds (2010) argues that, instead, we need to understand queer and trans relationships—including the multiple relationships queer and trans therapists engage in—within the context of their communities' experiences and ethics (without essentializing any of the above, of course). Questioning one-size-fits-all ethical codes that maintain dominant systems at the expense of local values, and local notions of ethical behavior, thus becomes a central tenet of relational responsibility (McNamee, 2009, 2015).

On top of all this, queer and trans therapists often face the increased scrutiny that is routinely applied to marginalized people. This extra surveillance (both from others and from a heteronormative story that a therapist may have absorbed) is understandably stressful on queer and trans therapists.

I've had many conversations with other queer and trans therapists about routine decisions that impact the quality of our lives: Do we avoid a bar or other venue that a client may frequent or work at? Do we not volunteer at an event for a community agency because we know that some of our clients will attend? Do we join a local gym that is queer-owned or queer-friendly, or will that involve too many overlapping relationships? If we do join, do we use the locker room and showers? Do we attend our neighbor's daughter's school play when we're the therapist to several queer and trans youth at the school? Do we forgo participating in social justice actions such as protests and marches? Can we publicly volunteer for a political campaign? While straight and cis therapists certainly face some variations of these questions now and then, queer and trans therapists have to regularly consider a great many of them.

Straight and Cisgender Therapists as Accomplices

If you're a straight and cis therapist, you may have felt left out of this chapter so far. Don't worry—I have a job for you: Use your privilege for good. Be an *accomplice* to the disruption of codes of conduct that challenge queer and trans community practices.

I use *accomplice* instead of *ally* because allyship implies the support of individuals. In contrast, accomplices provide more than just individual support. An accomplice (1) takes risks, (2) follows the lead of queer and trans people, and (3) demands accountability to queer and trans people. Accomplices challenge institutional and systemic injustices. In short, an accomplice:

- Critically questions (through self-reflexivity) their own assumptions about institutional rules and professional codes of conduct
- Follows queer and trans therapists' leads in changing and drafting policies about multiple relationships, and in providing consultation on navigating their multiple relationships
- Educates other straight and cis therapists about the normativity embedded within conventional ethics, as well as about the relationship practices and ethics in the queer and trans communities
- Directly challenges codes of conduct that denigrate or fail to comprehend queer and trans relationship practices.

As an accomplice, you can act as a buffer, responding to some of the flak that queer and trans therapists may get for advocating for multiple relationships. This might include disrupting clinical practices and organizational policies in the organization you work for. It may also involve pushing on professional organizations and governmental licensing boards.

In speaking out about, and working to change, a professional culture that often looks down on multiple relationships—or that fails to see the nuances involved in them—you take a risk. But in doing so, you serve your queer and trans colleagues—and a great many trans and queer clients.

Queer(ing) Ethics: More than Multiple Relationships

Being an accomplice to queer and trans therapists isn't the only ethical stance required of cis and straight therapists practicing queer theory-informed narrative therapy. And thoughtfully navigating multiple relationships isn't the only ethical matter for queer and trans therapists to consider. A larger shift is required—a shift from *ethical questions* to a practice of *ethics as questions*. This is the central practice of queering ethics.

As therapists, we encounter ethical questions whenever we address specific clinical situations that present challenges. For instance, is it ethical to accept a gift from a client? Or, is it ethical to report an undocumented immigrant family to child protection services? Is it ethical not to? What if you know that there is abuse in the family? What if you only suspect that there may be? Conventional professional ethics direct us to turn to our licensing body's codes of conduct and rules. But these guidelines won't do, because they provide formulaic responses to specific situations that are often anything but formulaic.

Alternatively, ethics as questions (Freedman & Combs, 1996) require an ongoing interrogation of our own practice. Ethics as questions encourage us to scrutinize not one particular event, but our entire practice in terms of its effects on people. Thus, we determine the ethicality of our actions based on how they impact the lives of the people we work with—not on our adherence to a professional or governmental code of conduct that was constructed elsewhere, far away from the particular people and situation.

Here are some examples of ethics as questions that can help you to queerly interrogate your practice:

- How does this model, theory, or practice "explain" people?
- How does this model, theory, or practice "explain" queer and trans people?
- How does it expect you to engage with the people you work with?
- How does it expect the people who seek your services to act with you?

- How would you describe the positioning—i.e., the positions you and your client take with one another—encouraged by this practice?
- Who is considered to have knowledge and expertise?
- Who enters whose world?
- Does this way of doing therapy foster normativity? Generativity?
- What are the effects of this practice on your clients? On their relationships with important other people in their lives? On the communities they belong to?
- What is valued in this model or theory? What is devalued or dis-valued?
- How is professionalism defined? Who gets to define it, and what values does this definition reflect?

(adapted from Freedman & Combs, 1996)

By asking critical questions about what we do—and more importantly, *what our doing does* (Foucault, 1965)—we can step into full accountability to the people who consult us.

Engaging with ethics as questions leads us to evaluate how our practices may impact particular people at a particular time, rather than relying on a one-size-fits-all approach. This allows us to be flexible and fluid in what our practices make possible—and what they close off—for our clients and their communities. McNamee (2009, 2015) calls this kind of responsiveness *relational responsibility* or *relational ethics*.

Queering ethics involves a shift from centering rules to centering relationships and our processes of interacting (Tilsen, 2018). McNamee (2009, 2015) suggests that this is a shift from a way of *doing* ethics to a way of *being* in relationship. It is a stance rather than a technique. When you approach ethics in this way, ethics become an everyday affair, rather than something you consider only in response to specific dilemmas or legal matters.[2]

In a queered therapy practice, we understand that when we talk about ethics, we are talking about power relations and how people are affected by power. This expanded view of ethics demands that we acknowledge that everything we do in our therapeutic relationships has ethical implications, even when no dilemma exists. We also acknowledge that there are too many worldviews to assume that there is only one true and right one—and that imposing a moral order from outside a given community on that community may, in some ways or situations, be unethical. This is why I say that *ethics are the blood that courses through the body of our work* (Tilsen, 2018).

I call this expanded view of ethics *everyday ethics*. Attending to everyday ethics means that we ask questions about many taken-for-granted practices and their effects. We examine the assumptions that uphold these practices. We expose power—where it is and where it isn't. We pave the way for the consideration of multiple perspectives and values.

Here are some starter questions for you to consider about some common practices, and the ethics that inform and perpetuate them:

- When meeting with an individual for a relational issue: *Who is assumed to bear responsibility for problems in the relationship?*
- When medicating someone who is struggling with depression and anxiety, which are responses to ongoing systemic oppression: *Where are we locating the problem(s) when we do this?*
- When providing supervision or consultation without the client present: *Who is seen as an authority on whose life?*
- When continuing therapy in a case where the client has experienced no change: *Who am I accountable to?*

These everyday clinical practices hold relevance beyond work with queer and trans clients, of course. The call to queer our ethics is a call that all therapists can and should answer, regardless of who they work with.

Not "Anything Goes": Queering Is Not Relativizing

If you think that I'm using a lot of space to say that everything we do and all the decisions we make are "relative," hold on. I'm not.

This is one of two common misunderstandings about (and arguments against) relational ethics. The second misunderstanding is that this perspective on ethics views all constructions and stories as equally valid. I'm not saying this, either. A flexible, responsive ethical stance is not about promoting rampant moral relativism that can justify any atrocity. There's a difference between considering alternate stories and validating every one of those stories. (Note the binary that's implied here by the normative discourse: *If you reject what is normative, you therefore accept—and equally value—every other possible discourse.*) Relational ethics are about de-centering and examining our own practices, not about relativizing situations and valuing all stories equally.

Here's what I am saying: queer ethics require that we focus on power relations, and on who has the authority to decide what is right. This creates space for—and requires us to consider—a variety of discourses and perspectives, not just the normative ones. This applies in many contexts, including those involving professional ethical codes. When working with marginalized people, such as queer and trans people, this is particularly vital.

Acknowledging and seeking to understand other ethical standpoints and worldviews does not require us to agree with them. However, it does require that we recognize that we are not the keepers of the One Right Way. As feminist ethicists and practitioners Hill, Glazer, and Harden (1998) point out, ethics have traditionally been the province of professionals, where client voices go not only unheard, but often uninvited.

Queering your ethics (and your practice) requires that you resist participating in the project of disciplinary power (Foucault, 1977) that elevates expert knowledge and suppresses all other ways of making meaning, knowing, and being. This does not mean anything goes; it means that nothing goes unquestioned.

Living into Our Values

Kat, a white 50-year-old cisgender lesbian, had been practicing family therapy for over 20 years. In consultation, she brought up her work with Erin and Ash, a lesbian couple whom she described as "white, cis, late 20s, and really radical." Kat said that she was having a hard time "living my values of respecting what they want, because it conflicts with my ideas of healthy relationships."

The tension lay between the couple's desire to "find a way to stay friends" as they ended their romantic relationship after five years, and Kat's "best clinical judgment that that's not good for either of them."

I asked Kat about her own values—what they were, who and what inspired them, what they said about what matters to her, and how they've changed over the years. I was also curious about when she felt best able to live into her own values. What and who made this possible? When this was difficult? What barriers did she see to living and embodying her values?

As we talked, Kat said that it's important to her to "listen to and honor women because of how they're disempowered and controlled by society." Kat explained that consulting with other feminist family therapists helps her stay close to this ethic. "They've taught me how to pay attention to the ways that women get shut down and controlled."

I was also curious about Kat's idea of "best clinical judgment." We discussed what informed this idea; how she determined what's "best"; and, most importantly, how this notion of her being the keeper of "best clinical judgment" squared with her ethical aspiration of honoring women and attending to the ways that they get silenced.

"That's exactly the problem," Kat said. "It doesn't square. But I keep having this negative reaction to their insistence that they can stay friends."

Kat explained that she was "getting drawn away from my own ethics, which make me want to tell them that I think they should have a clean break-up."

I asked Kat about the assumptions upholding this idea. I also asked her to examine and question the patriarchal and heteronormative implications of "the clean break-up." This conversation brought forward the tension between Kat's ethical aspirations and the normative ideas about relationships embedded within some of the ideas that informed her work.

Our conversation also exposed adultism as another prevailing discourse that was influencing her. Kat noted how she was "carrying this paternalistic idea that Ash and Erin are too young to know what's best for themselves." Then she said, "That's the kind of patriarchal bullshit I don't want to dump on anyone."

As a result of her insights from this conversation, Kat was able to find a way to share with the couple the questions she had about a future friendship in a way that "reflected my intention to support their successful relationship transition, not any traditional ideas about how to do it."

Kat's dilemma is an example of how we can easily stray from our own intended relational ethic. This *ethics drift* (Tilsen, 2018) is often a result of the powerful winds of prevailing discourses, both cultural and professional. My discussion with Kat demonstrates how we can right our course by unpacking these discourses and their effects on our practice. Once Kat questioned the assumptions embedded within these discourses, she was able to re-center and reclaim her feminist relational ethic.

Interrogating the power of cultural norms and professional practices in this way is central to queering ethics, to queering your practice, to living into relational responsibility, and to best assisting your clients.

Notes

1. *Two-spirit* refers to a person who identifies as having both a masculine and a feminine spirit. It is a term used by some people who are indigenous to what is known as North America.

2. More and more, legal issues have become conflated with ethical issues. As a sad result, today our professional ethics have become very much about avoiding legal problems and covering our asses.

5

QUEERING NARRATIVES, HONORING LIVES

Chicken Smarts

Thirteen-year-old Quinn, a cisgender BIPOC girl, settled into the chair next to me and reached for the candy jar. Her parents, Eric (a Black, straight, cisgender man) and Rachel (a white, straight, cisgender woman), sat on the loveseat across from us. The four of us had met a handful times before, and the family always came prepared to talk about any new developments and challenges they were addressing since Quinn had come out as bi. I enjoyed their humor and the affection they expressed for each other, and I especially appreciated how fiercely supportive and proud of Quinn Rachel and Eric were.

Eventually the conversation landed on the topic of, in Quinn's words, "coming out to more people at school." As Quinn talked, I heard an all-too-common refrain: "I'm just not brave enough to come out to them." I'd often heard both young people and adults disparage themselves for lacking the courage to come out to certain people. Of course, I had questions.

"Quinn," I asked, "what kinds of situations or experiences have you encountered in your life that required courage?"

"Well, I guess stuff that seems scary. Like when I auditioned for the musical. Also, when I told my teacher last year that he was wrong about something."

"OK, so stuff that seems scary requires some kind of courage…Is something at risk in those scary situations—something that matters to you?"

Quinn nodded. "With the teacher, I was afraid I'd get in trouble, or he'd say something to embarrass me. With the musical, I just really wanted to be in it with my friends. I didn't want to miss out."

I asked Quinn if I could check with her parents about when they'd seen her have courage, and she agreed.

Eric and Rachel talked about how they saw Quinn as being "very courageous, but not stupid."

"For example," Rachel said, "when Quinn was about eight, she told her best three friends that she wouldn't play with them anymore if they kept making racist comments about the Somali family that lives down the street….We weren't sure, to be honest, how these kids or their parents would react, and Quinn had literally grown up playing with these three little girls. They were tight, and she knew she could lose them, but she said it was OK because she had other friends who aren't mean."

Eric added, "That's what we mean by courageous but not stupid: it was a risk, but she understood what was at stake and had a back-up plan. She might end up hurt and sad, but she knew she'd be OK."

"OK," I said. "So, does she have smart courage, or courageous smarts?"

"Both!" Quinn half-shouted. Her parents nodded in agreement.

Eric said, "I also think she used smart courage when she came out to us. It was really brave to come out to us, but I hope for her it wasn't stupid. I mean, she knew we'd support her."

Quinn added, "I didn't feel brave coming out to you because it wasn't scary. I didn't think that anything bad would happen."

We talked for a few minutes about what this meant in terms of their connection, the trust among them, how well Rachel and Eric were living into their mission as parents, and the security Quinn experienced with them. Then I said, "So, if I have this right, stuff that's scary, where something bad could happen, requires courage. But stuff that isn't scary, and something bad can't happen—like coming out to your parents—doesn't require courage. Am I keeping up?"

"Barely!" Quinn said, then popped some candy in her mouth.

"Thank you for bearing with me." I smiled. "So, regarding coming out to everyone at school, how do you assess this situation—is it one that requires courage, or nah?"

"Totally. It's really scary," Quinn said seriously.

"And, would you say that you're using smart courage or courageous smarts, or both, or something else?"

"I don't know... I don't have any courage. I'm a chicken."

"Quinn, do smart courage and courageous smarts mean that you always do the thing that's scary and risky? I mean, what would stupid courage or courageous stupidity look like? Wait, maybe it's chicken smarts?"

Quinn paused. Then she laughed and looked at her parents. "I don't know....What do you mean by chicken smarts?"

"Well, I'm wondering a couple of things. First, in general, does having courage and smarts mean you always do something that's scary? And, I'm wondering if there's something smart about being chicken in this specific situation."

"Maybe...?" It was half a statement, half a question.

"OK, so, before you told your teacher he was wrong, you weighed the possibility of getting in trouble and decided it was worth it. Before you auditioned, you weighed the possibility of not being in the show and missing out on stuff with your friends. When you were little, you decided you could handle not being besties with those three friends anymore if they wouldn't shut down the racist stuff....Do I have this right, Quinn?"

"Uh-huh."

"So, Quinn, what's at stake that you're not willing to do without, or that you're deciding is not something you should have to go through, if you come out to everyone at school?"

"Well, I could get beat up, or teased, and all the stuff that straight people do to queer people. I go to a really conservative school."

"Quinn, are you saying that you're not willing to get beat up or teased or subjected to homophobic stuff?"

"I'm not stupid!"

"No, you're not. In fact, is this what chicken smarts might be?"

"Yeah, I guess so!" Quinn laughed.

"Quinn, if you're using chicken smarts to keep from getting beat up and stuff, does that mean you value your safety and dignity?"

"Well, yeah. I do. I never thought of it like that."

"Is it okay if I ask your parents some questions?"

"Sure," Quinn said.

I asked Eric and Rachel if they had any other stories about Quinn taking care of her own safety and dignity. They offered a few examples, and I asked them if they saw any connection between Quinn's history of keeping herself safe and how she was now protecting herself at school. They both did. "In every example" Rachel said, "Quinn chose her safety over what she would hope for someday—but other people or circumstances made it too dangerous for her, either physically or emotionally."

I asked Rachel, "So, you saw, and now see, Quinn staying away from danger?"

Rachel nodded. Eric said, "Totally."

"So, she's engaging in practices of protection?"

Eric's face opened in a smile. Rachel said, "Absolutely."

I turned back to Quinn. "So, what do you think about what your parents said? Are you engaging in practices of protection?"

Quinn's mouth fell open a little. Then the words "Yes, yes I am!" jumped out.

We continued talking about how chicken smarts, courageous smarts, and smart courage were all types of Quinn's practices of protection. Quinn also identified some other practices that she used at school, and out in the community, that involved friends and family helping her. She dubbed these people her "protection posse."

By the end of the conversation, Quinn decided that "I'm out to the people that I want to be out to, right now. I'm not going to win a medal if I tell every random kid at school."

We all agreed that this showed all kinds of smarts and courage—and that it was a testimony to Quinn's regard for her own worth.

As we wrapped up the session, Quinn pulled her phone out of her pocket and starting feverishly texting. Eric asked her to put the phone away until they left.

"Sorry," Quinn said. "I'm just texting Sonny, Bree, Jessi, and André to tell them that they're not chicken—they have chicken smarts!"

From Queer Narratives to Queering Narratives

When a 13-year-old queer girl (or, really, a queer or trans person of any age) collapses the identity of "chicken" onto themselves, my discursive landscape compass immediately points to the compulsory coming out narrative. This influential discourse comes out of various models of identity development[1] that position "coming out" as a targeted achievement and end point (Tilsen, 2013), in which queer and trans people ostensibly emerge from a universalized developmental trajectory, and are then whole and complete.

This narrative relies, first and foremost, on the individualistic notion of an essential self. According to this notion, there is an "authentic self" that develops within people, and this self includes their gender and sexuality (although, as we've seen, these categories are highly unstable). It also relies on the institutionalization of heterosexuality and cisgenderism. After all, there would be nothing for anyone to develop into and come out to if we didn't set cisness and straightness as defaults—and if gender and sexuality were not categories into which we sorted people.

In this chapter, I provide some queer critiques of this pervasive discourse. I offer an alternative queer theory-informed narrative therapy approach to working with this important issue. And I critique another prevalent (and related) narrative: *the parental loss narrative*. As with the coming out narrative, I provide alternative ways to engage people around this idea of "losing a child[2]" when that child comes out.

Q-TIPS: NARRATIVE THERAPY IN ACTION

In my conversation with Quinn and her parents, I did a good deal of deconstructing and asking meaning-making questions. I'd like you to read that vignette again, and identify some of the narrative therapy practices that I used.

Here are a few examples:

- **Absent but implicit:** I asked Quinn about what was on the other side of the scariness she experienced—that is, what mattered to her—when she considered coming out to someone. This paved the way for our conversation about protecting what matters to her
- **Externalizing:** I externalized chicken smarts, smart courage, courageous smarts, and practices of protection, rather than locating them internally, as Quinn's characteristics or attributes
- **Multiple perspectives:** I sought Rachel and Eric's input. This provided not only a variety of perspectives, but also a history that enabled us to connect Quinn's current courageous smarts and smart courage to her past actions and decisions.

Coming In from Coming Out

In general, therapists—queer and cis, straight and trans—are trained to encourage coming out. Yet our cultural and professional infatuation with the individualistic ideal of "being yourself" can obscure the unique complexities surrounding any person's coming out and being out. Although this stance is well-intentioned, assuming that stance is potentially problematic.

To begin with, compulsory coming out can function as a standard that people feel obligated to uphold. This often sows the seeds for feelings of failure, as people evaluate themselves and feel that they are not coming out in the "right way." Quinn was caught up in self-evaluation because she felt that she was failing a standard of being totally out to everyone.

A second problem is the implication that *not* coming out represents internalized homophobia, and is dishonest, and lacks courage—that is, that if a person chooses not to come out to everyone, they're broken or bad in some way. For example, recall the story of Cesar from Chapter 2. His white American friends accused him of internalized homophobia and of not being honest with himself. Yet they ignored important cultural contexts that involved not only Cesar's physical safety, but also the safety of his connections with family. This was an ill-suited and ill-advised standard for coming out. LaTrisha (from Chapter 1) also faced allegations of internalized homophobia, because she took a stand against identity labels and categories. In short, compulsory coming out perpetuates the burden of individualism and the privatization of social problems by placing the responsibility of coming out on individual persons, while ignoring both context and personal meaning-making.

Discourses around honesty in coming out are especially problematic—and especially powerful. I often hear people say, "I don't want to lie about who I am." I also hear therapists say that they want to encourage people "to be honest about who they are." Of course, I am not advocating dishonesty or lying. I *am* saying that the honest/dishonest binary, like most binaries, is limiting. It ignores context, and it values one of only two acceptable and recognized positions (in this case, honesty) over the other.

For an alternative way to approach the notion of honesty, we can turn to Foucault's (1997) ideas about what he calls *games of truth*. Foucault defines truth games as "a set of rules by which truth is produced" (p. 197). According to Foucault, truth is socially constructed, and both produced by and productive of power relations. When we participate in games of truth, we engage in self-subjugation and self-policing that are indistinguishable from the policing of identity by dominating discourses, institutions, systems, structures, and people. The compulsory coming out discourse becomes a truth game when people's primary or sole purpose for coming out is a response to this pressure to "be honest."

When I explore this with clients, I inquire about their relationship with honesty, and why it's something they value. This enables them to honor and thicken the story of their relationship with honesty. I also ask questions that situate their experience in discourse. This positions us to consider how "failing at honesty"[3] might also mean resisting unjust or dishonest expectations. It might also mean succeeding at maintaining dignity, practices of protection, or something else that matters.

Here are some sample questions I might ask a client as we deconstruct discourses of honesty:

- Can you tell me about your history with honesty, and what about it matters to you?
- Who has inspired your relationship with honesty?
- Who else can relate stories about your relationship with honesty?
- Could there be situations when there's something other than honesty or dishonesty involved—where there are some complexities or nuances? What examples of such situations can you think of, either from your own experience or the experience of others?
- Do you think all people always respect the truths of others? Has everybody always respected your truth?
- Given how much you value honesty, how do you decide who deserves your truth, and who does not?
- What might be the relationship between considerations of honesty/dishonesty and practices of protection?
- Think again about the people you know who can speak of your relationship with honesty. What advice do you think they would give you about coming out—and about honesty—in situations that you see as unsafe?
- If not coming out in a particular situation is dishonest, does this make you a liar? Does it erase all the times you've been honest?
- Is it fair or just to consider yourself or someone else a "liar" if they choose to engage in practices of protection?
- Do you think that a world that assumes cisness and straightness is honest in making those assumptions?
- If the assumption of cisness and straightness is not honest, then how is it that you and other trans or queer people end up as dishonest—or as liars?

Stories of being liars, and/or of lacking courage, place the problems of homophobia and transphobia squarely on the shoulders of queer and trans people. The questions in the list above, and others like them, free people from this unjust burden by situating the issue of coming out in discourse. They also challenge the binaries of honest/dishonest and courageous/cowardly, and situate them not as essential qualities of a person, but as relational acts. Each such act occurs within, and is influenced by, the discourse—as well as by the politics and the ethics of the particular relationship involved.

What are the implications for your therapy practice? By situating honesty and courage in discourse—and understanding them as relational activities rather than as essential, internal characteristics—we are better positioned to help people generate thick, contextualized stories. For Quinn, understanding what she was doing as "practices of protection" and "chicken smarts" (practices that had both a history and appreciative witnesses) freed her from the thin and problem-saturated identity conclusion that she lacked courage. These practices then became available to Quinn as important skills that she could use again, as she saw fit.

When people who are tangled up in truth games have a chance to question the idea of "being honest," they often tell stories that involve practices of protection and taking care of relationships. There are other practices, too, that can help people navigate the complexities and contradictions that this issue is thick with. For example, Randy—a white, cis, gay man from a fundamentalist Christian family—said to me, "Not everyone deserves my truth, because they'll distort it to hurt me and others." Randy's pronouncement is as clear a comment on the politics of truth as I've ever heard.

While claiming a queer identity can be enormously powerful and liberating for some people, coming out "is not an equal-opportunity endeavor" (Tilsen & Nylund, 2010). For example, the consequences of coming out and being out are different for me as an older, middle-class, white, cisgender professional living in the United States than they may be for people who occupy other social locations—or for people with less financial stability or less access to support and resources. This is another critical reason for taking up an intersectional approach.

Given the contexts of heteronormativity, homonormativity, and cisnormativity, visibility is undeniably important for queer and trans people. This means that, as a therapist, you need to reconcile the tension between queer theory's questioning of mandatory identity practices (e.g., fixed categories and compulsory coming out) and the personal and collective political power that people experience through coming out (Tilsen, 2013).

Cultural theorist Jack (formerly Judith) Halberstam (2005) queers the process and trajectory of the conventional coming out narrative and offers a useful stance for this dilemma. Halberstam suggests that, rather than coming out being an *end point*, it is a *starting point* from which we ask the question, *Now what?* Other questions naturally follow: *In what ways might your identity continue to unfold or emerge from this place? What does being out make possible for you and others? How can you use your outness to challenge the constraints of normativity?* Embracing coming out as *a collective practice that cultivates community*, rather than as an individual task to accomplish, is one way to re-imagine and re-organize our relationship with coming out. In doing so, we help generate, make available, and welcome in an abundance of nuanced and situated stories. One or more of these can then be selected and lived into.

Conversations such as these signal our recognition of both the constructive and the problematic aspects of coming out. They also help us to have complex and generative conversations with our clients about meaningful futures.

We can understand coming out as a political reality in a heteronormative, homonormative, and cisnormative world, while simultaneously fostering resistance to the oppressive realities that make coming out a perceived necessity.

Ultimately, what matters is that we approach coming out with a critical curiosity; an openness to a variety of ways people make meaning of it; and conceptual and conversational resources that question the effects of coming out or not coming out.

Q-TIPS: REFLECTING ON COMING OUT

Consider these questions (with a conversational partner or by yourself) about coming out:

- How have you thought about coming out?
- What position do you take with clients on coming out?
- How does intersectionality influence your thoughts about coming out?

- Do you think straight and cis people should practice routine coming out?
- What's new for you to consider? What's challenging? What new possibilities are emerging for you?

What does all of this look like in the therapy room? In addition to having conversations about practices of protection and resisting dishonest demands for honesty, I have conversations about *inviting people in* (Beckett, 2007; Tilsen, 2013). Extrapolating on White's (1997) idea of each of us having a *club of life* (in which we choose whom we invite into our lives and who merits a high-status membership, based on how much we value their influence), I ask questions such as these:

- Who would you like to invite into your life, where you can be a gracious host—rather than coming out into a hostile world that treats you as an unwelcome stranger?
- How do people qualify for a platinum-level membership in the club of your life? A gold-level membership? A silver? A bronze?
- What are disqualifiers—things that prevent people from being invited in?
- What will people discover when you invite them in that isn't available to them from the outside?
- What difference do you imagine (or have you experienced) inviting people in will make, compared to when you come out?
- Who do you get to be when you've hand-selected who you invite in? How does this compare to whom you get to be when you feel pressured to come out?

Shifting the conversation from coming out to inviting others in puts people in charge of their own stories and processes. It also undoes the all-or-nothing, in-the-closet/out-of-the-closet binary that's at least implicit, and often explicit, in the conventional coming out narrative. Thus, we create space for the relationship complexities, nuances, and contradictions that most people live with.

Critiquing the compulsory coming out narrative does not imply that it is universally and categorically wrong. For some people, surely, it is useful and relevant. My purpose here is not to completely devalue a dominating discourse, but to critique it—and to remind you that such a critique makes visible what has been obscured by the very domination of that discourse. In other words, we critique influential discourses in order to stay mindful of the assumptions that uphold them—and to acknowledge that these discourses do not include or apply to everyone. This is one way we can stay close to our clients' experiences—and avoid participating in games of truth and other dominating practices.

Q-TIPS: RESISTING THE BINARY OF SUPPORTIVE/ NOT SUPPORTIVE

How often do you say (or think) that someone is either supportive or not supportive of a queer or trans person? This is an easy binary to fall into, but one that is very important for therapists to unpack. If we don't, we run the risk of overlooking meaningful nuances—and missing opportunities to nurture relationships between queer and trans people and the significant people in their lives.

Support is not an all-or-nothing thing; it almost always happens in degrees. There are a variety of ways of expressing support. For example, a parent may not understand or support their trans or nonbinary child's desire for gender affirmation surgery, but they may use their child's chosen name and respect their pronouns. Or, a gay man's sister may not be willing to go to a gay drag show with him at a gay bar, but she may welcome him and his boyfriend into her home.

Finding points of support—even imperfect or partial support—is important for starting conversations, and for keeping them going. Allowing support to occur in steps, or to unfold over time, respects the complexity of support, focuses on relationships, and provides an opportunity for queer and trans people to experience greater affirmation from significant people in their lives.

Say Goodbye to the Parental Loss Narrative

Jen and Owen, both straight, cisgender, and white, were the parents of their five-year-old gender-creative trans daughter, C.J. Owen and Jen met with me to talk about some questions they were grappling with around parenting C.J.

After our initial introductions, I asked if I could "meet" C.J. through some pictures or videos they had on their phones. Jen showed me a video of C.J. wearing purple tights, a long, polka-dot t-shirt, and a blinged-out tiara. C.J. was singing the theme from Frozen, punctuating the high notes with dramatic, full-body gestures. "C.J. loves theatrics," Owen said, laughing.

The couple shared how C.J., who was assigned male at birth, first told them that she was a girl when she started pre-school a year earlier. They decided at the time to, as Jen said, "give him some room, not force anything." She described trying to make available all kinds of clothes and toys for C.J., "so that his stuff didn't have to be gendered."

Owen added, "We wanted him to get the idea that there's not a right way to be a boy, and that he could be any kind of a boy he wanted to be—including a boy who likes and does what some people think are girl things."

"The thing is," Jen said, "C.J. isn't any kind of boy. She's a girl. And it took us almost a year to really believe her."

As we talked, it was clear that Jen and Owen were advocating fiercely for C.J. They had set clear expectations with extended family members about pronouns and C.J.'s name. (They were using the initials of her given name until C.J. decided she wanted to change her name.) They made sure that play dates validated C.J.'s female gender. They made sure that C.J.'s school was supportive of gender-creative and trans children, in both its policies and its practices. It was clear to me that Owen and Jen were as responsive as possible to their child's needs. They had also connected with some other parents of trans and gender-creative children for perspective and support.

Yet, while doing what they needed to do for C.J., Owen and Jen found themselves struggling with some conflicting feelings. "We absolutely know we're doing what's best for C.J.," Owen said. (Jen nodded her agreement.) "But sometimes one of us, or both of us, feels sad about it. It's not about worry or fear about the challenges she'll face—that's real, and something to talk about sometime, for sure. This is something different than that."

Jen added, "Yeah, it's like, we see how absolutely happy she is now, and how it hurts her if someone misgenders her. It feels like a selfish thing we both get caught up in. It's a kind of disappointment, like we've lost the little boy we had...or thought we had."

They both explained that they felt bad about feeling bad. They wanted to celebrate the happiness and freedom that C.J. was experiencing, but they weren't able to. Owen said, "Some people, including my own therapist, tell us it's natural to feel this way, and that it's a loss we need to grieve. But both Jen and I go back and forth on that."

The discourse that Owen named—the discourse of parental loss—receives less attention in the professional literature than the coming out discourse. Yet it influences many queer and trans people, many of their parents, and many of their therapists. In fact, when I do trainings or consultations, I'm often asked how to address "parental grief and loss."

Understandably, this discourse seems to matter a great deal to therapists. Bull and D'Arrigo-Patrick (2018) reviewed the family therapy literature and called the prevalence of this discourse "striking" (p. 174). A somewhat parallel review of the literature marketed to the parents of gay, lesbian, and bisexual children (Martin, Hutson, Kazyak, & Scherrer, 2010) reveals an extensive history of equating coming out as queer "to the death of a loved one" (Bull & D'Arrigo-Patrick, 2018, p. 174).

Many self-help books treat the emergence of a child's queer identity as, at best, disappointing to parents and, often, as tragic. Both the professional and lay literature cite Kubler-Ross's stages of grief as a framework for "working through" and "incorporating" the "loss" of a child who is queer or trans. One study of families with a transgender family member used the concept of *ambiguous loss* to explore people's reactions to having someone in the family come out as trans (Norwood, 2012).

Bull and D'Arrigo-Patrick (2018) acknowledge that some parents do experience feelings of grief and loss when their child announces their queer or trans identity. However, they also suggest that questioning the prevalence of the parental loss discourse in the professional literature (and the assumptions that undergird it) is necessary, so that therapists can avoid centering that discourse or imposing it on clients.

The parental loss narrative assumes straightness and cisness as defaults. To see this more clearly, let's return to my conversation with Jen and Owen. During our discussion, I strove to take a both/and approach, in which I honored and validated their feelings, and also asked questions that invited them to examine where those feelings came from. This is of course a queer approach; it's relational rather than individual in multiple ways. It locates feelings in the social world (i.e., in discourse) rather than views them as an internal state. It approaches gender transition as a family experience that involves all members and their relationships with each other. It questions norms. And it challenges one of therapy's most sacred cows: the exalted status of feelings.

Here is how my conversation with Owen and Jen continued:

JULIE: When it "feels like a loss," I'm wondering what has gone missing, or is no longer present in your lives, that's important to you, that you value?

JEN: I guess it's the ideas I had about who C.J. is, or who she would become. The idea that C.J. is a boy. That's what's gone.

OWEN: When you ask that, I think, *Well, what have we lost, actually? C.J. is still C.J.* But I still feel it…

JULIE: Yeah, that feeling is strong. It keeps a hold on you?

OWEN: Yes, very much.

JULIE: Owen, Jen said it's the *idea* about C.J. being a boy that's lost. Does that fit for you, too—that there's something about that idea that's lost, and that's what keeps you feeling it?

OWEN: Yeah, it's like you organize around some sense of what it means to have a boy or a girl, even when you try to avoid all the stereotypical gender crap, like we did. We didn't want all the problems that come with the idea. But maybe there's something comforting in the idea that your kid's gender is what it is.

JULIE: Jen, I see you nodding. What's Owen touched on that resonates for you? Can you say what's wrapped up in that idea that feels important, and speaks to what feels like it's lost?

JEN: It's just this really fundamental idea of having a boy or having a girl. But we're not invested in traditional "boy things" or "girl things," so I just swim in the feeling of sadness, of loss, even though it doesn't make logical sense.

JULIE: Yeah, it doesn't make sense, given the critique you have of gender, right? And all the ways you've responded to C.J.'s gender-expansive interests and inclinations speak to your resistance to those norms. But the sadness is still there….Am I getting this?

JEN AND OWEN: Yes.

JULIE: OK, I want to make sure I understand this sadness and how it shows up, even though you've been so intentional around avoiding gender conventions. It sounds really painful. I'd like to ask some more about the idea of having a boy or having a girl. This might sound silly, but I'm really interested in understanding something—where does that idea come from? I mean, what set you up to have this fundamental idea, as Jen said, that you had a boy?

OWEN: Silly or not, that's a good question…

JEN: Yeah, it does feel like a set-up. It's everything that we're led to believe about gender…

OWEN: You know, the first question is always, "Is it a boy or girl?," and people buy stuff based on gender…

JEN: Yeah, it's like people have an idea that they can know something about a person, or a baby, by knowing the gender. And of course, the assumption is that we can even know the gender without the person having a say in it.

JULIE: OK, so there's all this stuff we do culturally that pressures us to identify gender, plus the assumption that a gender identity tells us something about the person. Plus, that someone's gender can be known independent of their having a say in it....Are there other assumptions that contributed to this set-up, and to the feelings of loss?

JEN: Well, the obvious one: that it's a girl or a boy based on their body, and that it will stay that way.

JULIE: Yeah. So, you mean it's a set-up for parents to assume that gender is based on anatomy? And that there only are boys and girls?

OWEN: Yeah, like, I knew it intellectually, and I know Jen did, too, but it was just an abstract idea. We weren't prepared for the possibility that our kid would be gender-creative and trans.

JULIE: What *were* you prepared for?

JEN: We were prepared to have a cisgender child who conformed to what we assumed her gender was, according to her body.

JULIE: How has your preparation for a cisgender child, and lack of preparation for a trans child, contributed to the sadness and loss you're experiencing?

JEN: Totally. I mean, that's it.

OWEN: Yeah, and that's why it doesn't feel right to feel this. We're losing an idea that's false anyway.

JEN: It's false and hurtful. I know it hurts C.J. to think that we're sad or missing something when she's so happy.

In this conversation, you can see that I took care to understand and validate Jen and Owen's experience, while I also asked questions to deconstruct their feelings. Understanding parents' feelings of grief and loss as products of discourse (rather than as "natural" internal states) shows compassion for parents. At the same time, situating loss *within* discourse gives parents discursive space to see that their experience is not their fault. This helps to alleviate the guilt that some parents feel.

Parents of queer and trans people did not ask for the gender binary, heteronormativity, or gender essentialism to shape their expectations and experiences of parenthood. When parents see how gender's cultural position as a powerful construct—one central to how we organize identities—contributes to their experience of loss, they can position themselves in relation to gender in ways that allow them to live into their values as parents.

In my work with clients, once the parental loss experience is deconstructed, I encourage the de-centering of gender (or sexuality, if that's the case), and uncouple it from what parents love about their child. Gender and sexuality are not typically what parents love about their children. Indeed, when I ask parents what they cherish, admire, enjoy, or love about their kids, they typically point to their children's actions, achievements, and ways of being in the world. I have never heard a parent say, "I love my child because they are a girl (or a boy)" or "We love our kids because they're straight." Through further deconstruction, we can detach personal qualities from gender or sexual identities—and, in the process, reveal the influence of discourse on constructing these specifications.

Q-TIPS: PARENTAL LOSS DISCOURSE AND THE DIFFERENCE BETWEEN SEXUALITY AND GENDER

There are actually two parallel parental loss discourses: one about a child's sexuality (whom they are attracted to) and one about their gender (how they define and describe themselves, and what they experience themselves to be). It's of course possible to have to grapple with both discourses in regard to the same child. Let's look at how these two discourses are similar—and how they diverge.

Both involve unmet expectations established by normative discourses: heteronormativity when a child's sexuality is queer, and cisnormativity when a child is transgender. As therapists, we can help our clients deconstruct these responses, and expose the assumptions of heteronormativity or cisnormativity wrapped inside them.

However, the effects of these two normative discourses tend to be quite different. While I frequently hear parents of queer people express a loss, I never hear them say, "I could handle this if they were trans." However, I often hear parents of trans people say, "This is really hard—I could handle it if they were gay." This speaks to the way that gender is seen as an immutable and natural attribute, while sexuality is not. And when something we thought was permanent changes, we are likely to experience a significant loss. (Of course, queer theory demands that we interrogate the discourses that circulate stories of gender as immutable.)

Then there is the conflation of anatomy with gender identity. Parents often focus on what a transgender identity means in terms of their child's body. Because trans and nonbinary people sometimes medically change their bodies so they can feel more at home in them, parents' feelings of loss can be a response to a gut-level reaction to the idea of making physical changes. Bodily adaptations seem more "real" in a world where corporeal matters are privileged. This gender essentialism, coupled with the cultural power of gender as fundamental to identity, produces the perfect discursive context for parents to feel a significant loss. They feel that the very "essence" of their child is changing—along with, perhaps, the body that houses that essence.

Compare this with essentialist discourses about sexual orientation (e.g., born this way; biological and genetic explanations; etc.). While these are also dominant, and widely accepted and assumed, parents may not feel as heavy a loss when their kids come out as queer, because this does not involve a body modification.

In addition, the success of the contemporary gay rights movement's core message—"We're just like you"—has blurred the difference between queers and straights. Queer people are now far more widely accepted by mainstream culture than they were only a generation ago. As of 2021, however, trans people have not received this wide acceptance. Thus, part of the trans parental loss discourse includes feeling that a child's inclusion in mainstream culture has been lost.

For example, Owen and Jen said that they always admired C.J.'s "confidence in her physical strength and abilities." While these particular qualities are traditionally gendered as male, Jen and Owen rejected that sexist coding. Instead, they embraced C.J.'s physicality as a "reflection of her passion for life and feeling good in her body." As they identified the many other things they cherished about C.J., I invited them to share stories around each of their daughter's qualities—the histories and possible futures of C.J's skills and attributes—so that they could imbue C.J and her abilities with meanings other than those organized around gender.

Another practice I use when working with parents is interviewing them about their mission as parents. A Mission Interview helps parents take a bird's-eye view of their parenting by focusing on their values and aspirations *as parents*. This gives parents an opportunity to reclaim what matters to them, and to reposition themselves in resistance to ideas that don't align with their own values, or with their hopes for their children.

For Jen and Owen, the Mission Interview (which we did in our second meeting) allowed them to reclaim their priority of "caring for C.J. and fostering her independence and happiness." After naming their mission and identifying the principles and practices that support it, Owen and Jen came to see the cisnormativity of the parental loss discourse as a barrier to their mission. As Jen said, "Supporting and celebrating C.J.'s health and happiness is at the heart of our mission. Anything that reinforces cisness takes away from her joy and doesn't align with our mission." This helped free them from the feelings of loss.

Below are some examples of questions I might ask in a Mission Interview:

- What is your mission, purpose, or aspiration as parents or (if my client is a single parent) a parent)? If you were to write a mission statement, what would that be?
- What is the history of this Mission? Who inspired it, and how?
- What experiences have you had in your life that helped shape this Mission?
- What values and principles inform this Mission?
- What are the practices you engage in that bring these values and principles to life?
- How will you know if you've accomplished your Mission?
- What are some of the barriers to living into your Mission?
- How do the conventions of gender and sexuality support your Mission? How do they thwart or complicate it?
- Who supports you in your Mission as parents? Who helps you live into it when these barriers get in your way?

- What would your child say have been some of your greatest Parenting Mission successes?
- What advice would they have for you to better live into your Mission?
- When you are really nailing your Mission, and parenting according to its values and principles, how much do the rules of normative gender and sexuality matter?
- What would you advise parents of a queer or trans child to do to help keep themselves focused on their Mission?

Mission interviews solidify parents' commitments to their children, and to their preferred identities as parents.

Sometimes, the questions I ask in a Mission interview help parents put words to—and reclaim—intentions and practices that they already center in their lives, but may have lost sight of in the struggle to make sense of their experience of their child's sexuality and gender identity. At other times, the questions evoke responses that parents say they had never felt or considered before. This is the magic of words—the *abracadabra* of language: the ability to create new, significant meanings that help people imagine and live into stories that matter.

Queering Narratives and Narrating Queerly

Let me say it again: the conventional discourses of coming out and parental loss can be meaningful, legitimate, and well-suited to many queer and trans people and their families. But they do not define the limits of legitimacy or meaning.

As a therapist, accepting these discourses without question puts you at risk of imposing unhelpful and possibly harmful narratives on people. It also prevents you from bringing out important nuances that lend meaning to people's lives.

Queering these narratives involves questioning the previously unquestioned assumptions and the discourses they uphold. It also involves helping people to story their lives in ways that not only resist convention, but *honor* this lack of convention, in all its contradictions and complexities.

Notes

1. The emergence, acceptance, and integration of a gay, lesbian, bisexual, or transgender identity is known variously as *identity development* (Coleman, 1981–1982), *identity formation* (Cass, 1984), *identity acquisition* (Troiden, 1979), or *differential developmental trajectories* (Savin-Williams, 1998; Savin-Williams & Diamond, 1997), depending on the model used.
2. I use "child" and "children" to define a relationship, not to distinguish age. In other words, my use of child/children is inclusive of queer and trans adults in relationship with their parents.
3. I draw on Halberstam's (2011) idea of the *queer art of failure* here. "Failing" to do something that is unhelpful, unmeaningful, or otherwise problematic is actually an art, given the pressure to doing or complete it.

6

SEXUAL HEALING

Sex Critical Practice

Sex Ed: Masculinity, Movies, and Media

Forty-two-year-old Logan was a tall, well-muscled, and well-tattooed straight cisgender white man who radiated confidence, energy, and warmth. In our first meeting, he told me that his therapy goal was to "help me be a better partner. I'm in a relationship that means the world to me; we see a future together; and I don't want to screw it up." He explained that he and his partner, Crystal (a 44-year-old Asian-American, straight, cisgender woman) had been together for two years, and that they have "always had different sexual interests and appetites."

I asked him to describe these differences. Even before he spoke, though, a heteronormative assumption appeared in my brain about who had a bigger sexual appetite and a more varied palate—Logan, the man. I cast aside the assumption and focused on listening.

"I've always kind of been, like, I can take it or leave it when it comes to just SEX." Logan emphasized the word with a big gesture. "And that makes me different than most men. Crystal's way more adventurous and generally just wants to have sex more than I do." He wanted help in "upping my sex game."

I asked him, "How have you come to think you're different from most men?"

Logan explained that, when he was younger, he felt that he had to choose between "making shit up about being horny and getting laid all the time" or being "teased by other guys if I was honest about my interest and level of sexual activity." Essentially, Logan said, he learned to "tell tall tales to be one of the guys" and avoid the taunting. "It helps," he added, "that I'm a pretty big guy and I weight train and rock climb, so other men look at me and make all kinds of ridiculous stereotypical assumptions."

We talked about some of the ways that hegemonic masculinity played a role in his idea that he needed to be a better partner by upping his sex game. Logan said, "Messages about masculinity do get into my head, even though I know they're bullshit—and Crystal tells me they're bullshit, too. It's like I got all my sex ed through movies and stuff."

I asked Logan to tell me some of the specific messages about masculinity that he felt were influencing him. He nodded and said, "Men should always want sex and be automatically good at it. You're not a real man if you don't always want sex. And it doesn't count as sex if you don't orgasm."

I asked Logan to describe his vision of a masculinity that suited him and the kind of sexual partner he aspired to be. He paused and thought for a few seconds, then said, "I really enjoy being sexual with Crystal, and I know it enhances our relationship. So, for me, being a man in this relationship means I do my part to help with the enhancement. I also really want and need other kinds of affection and connection with her. I want to be communicative about that—and attentive, thoughtful, and responsible. That's what it means to me to be a man. That's why I'm here talking to you."

"What have you and Crystal done together that's worked to enhance the relationship, even though there are these differences?" I asked.

Logan said, "I'm always willing to try things and Crystal's fine with masturbating and using porn when I'm not game. We both give a little. We listen to what each other cares about."

"Would you say that these are some ways that you're communicative, attentive, thoughtful, and responsible? That you're doing your part in enhancing the relationship?"

Logan agreed that he was living into his aspirations, and he said that the differences in their sexual desires hadn't created any problems in their relationship. Still, Logan was dogged by the idea that "there's something wrong with me." He felt guilty that Crystal was sacrificing more than he was. He added, "Crystal has never shamed or guilted me about this—it's all me. But I have this idea that I might lose her if I don't do more. In fact, she's more concerned that I worry about these things than that I don't match her sexual interest."

I asked Logan what Crystal might say she wants from a sexual partner; in what ways he meets that mark; and in what ways he misses it. He said, "Crystal feels more than satisfied with our relationship, including sexually. Like I said, it's me, and some of these ideas we've touched on that are stuck in my head."

I asked Logan how these ideas incited self-doubt and stirred up worries that his sexual participation in their relationship would be its downfall.

Logan talked about the ideas of masculinity he'd absorbed, plus what he'd seen in movies and other media, and how these had influenced him. We started calling these 3M: masculinity, movies, and media.

I asked Logan, "If you could write a guide entitled 'How to Have a Totally Normal and Successful Long-term Relationship with Your Life Partner According to 3M,' what would be some of the most important things that guide would tell you to do?"

Logan answered with a long list of items, all of them involving sex. These included: (1) it's bad for the relationship if you're not having sex, (2) you need to make sure sex is always really hot, (3) you should have sex at least three times a week, and (4) you need to try new sexual things often, so that you don't get stale and burn out on each other.

I asked Logan if he would consider inviting Crystal to our next meeting, and if he thought she would want to join us to offer her perspective. He laughed and said, "She was pretty frustrated that I insisted on doing this alone. She sees this as a we issue, not a me issue."

I asked, "Logan, do you take all the credit for the things that go well in your relationship?"

"No! That would be pretty arrogant and totally unreasonable."

"Is going it alone when there's a problem or concern your idea of 'reasonable'? Or is it part of 3M's agenda, to have you man up and fix this by yourself?"

"Yeah, it's totally 3M for me to try to do this myself without Crystal. This conversation has me thinking that 3M has way too much say over me right now."

"Sounds like there's a lot of extra voices in the conversation about your sexual relationship with Crystal. Have either of you asked for 3M's advice?"

"No! It's like there are a hundred other people in our bedroom telling me what I should do. Neither of us asked for that. I want 3M out of my head, my relationship, my bedroom. Count us both in for next time."

Although we're told that sex is "natural," my conversation with Logan illustrates just how strongly our understandings of sex (and our efforts to participate in it) are embedded in and influenced by culture. We have countless narratives about what constitutes a "normal," "healthy," and "successful" relationship, and a "normal," "healthy," and "successful" sex life. (Note how the reflexive pairing of relationship and sex life points to one of those narratives.) All of these discourses shape people's ideas of who they're supposed to be, and who they are. Regardless of what kind of formal sex education we received in school, our sexual attitudes, ideas, and practices are shaped by cultural discourses, just as Logan's were. Our conversation exposed not only normative ideas of masculinity, but also the prevailing cultural narratives about what constitutes a "normal" or "healthy" relationship, particularly in regard to sex.

Pointing a critical, queered lens toward these matters not only makes visible the dominating discourses; it also shines light in previously shadowed spaces, helping us and our clients navigate toward meaningful, preferred relationships with sex.

Let's take a closer look at how queering our approach to sex opens up these possibilities for everyone, regardless of their gender or sexual identities, preferences, and practices.

Not as Natural as You Think

It's helpful to start with a quick review of how sex is socially constructed and what the effects of these constructions are on our lives.

You'll recall from Chapter 1 the discussion of Foucault's (1978) history of the invention of homosexuality (and its twin sibling, heterosexuality). This is important as we address sex, inasmuch as sex went from what we do (i.e., our sexual practices) to what we do *and* who we are (our sexual identities or orientations, based on our sexual practices). Acknowledging these categories as social constructs defies the popular notion that sex is "simply natural" and that sexual identities are immutable, essential characteristics. Certainly, we have desires and inclinations in regard to sex and pleasure that *just are* what we like. But the *meanings* we ascribe to these desires, and the *stories* that circulate about them, are very much situated in discourse and culture. Or, as I like to say, if sex is so natural, how come we have sex education?

For example, in 21st-century North American culture, the frequency of sex that Logan prefers is viewed as problematic, especially for men. Logan acted according to his preferred level of interest in sex, but he was well aware of the cultural stories packed with expectations that he "up his game" to be a "real man." Furthermore, Logan was dismissive of his preference for physical affection and activities that he defined as "not really sex." As we talked, I discovered that what he meant was that, while he enjoyed a lot of non-genital activities with Crystal such as making out, giving each other massages, and showering together, he had come to learn that these activities don't count as sex—and that it mattered whether something counted as sex or not.

How did he learn this? Through discourse, of course.

Let's consider some other examples of how our so-called "natural" sexual inclinations are situated within and influenced by discourse:

- Joci is a woman who has an affinity for frequent sex with many partners. What are the cultural stories about her? How do these stories change if the woman is white, Black, or Asian? How do the stories change if she is 20 years old or if she is 60? If she is cisgender or trans, able-bodied or disabled?

- Jeremiah has never had much interest in sex and experiences no sexual attraction to other people. Having found some grounding in the identity of asexual (ACE), Jeremiah now experiences a tremendous amount of scrutiny and doubt from other people, who can't believe that any "normal, healthy" person would have no interest in sex. In addition to the sex-is-natural discourse, what other narratives shape people's perceptions of and reactions to someone who is ACE? What are some of the common discourses within psychotherapy about people who are not interested in sex? How do these discourses vary based on gender, race, physical ability, class, and/or age?

- Consider our discourses around youth and sex. In The Netherlands, teen sex is understood to be a normal and healthy aspect of growing up. Dutch youth receive explicit sexual health education that focuses on being responsible in relationships. They are encouraged by their parents and other adults to engage in the "natural" act of sex as caring and responsible partners who are seeking pleasure (Schalet, 2011). Compare this to the way teen sex is constructed in the United States, where young people learn little or nothing about pleasure, or about being responsible in sexual relationships. American sex ed tends to focus heavily on abstinence, pregnancy prevention, and STI avoidance (Tilsen, 2013). In fact, in the United States, teen sex is considered to be a "risk factor," something to prevent and avoid (deVries, 2008).

- Consider how monogamous marriage—although clearly a troubled institution, according to divorce statistics—is heralded as the gold standard of relationships. (Also, note how we assume that marriage is—thanks to the dominating discourse—invariably a sexual relationship!) Next to marriage, long-term relationships are valued, although we never say how long is long-term. How did we come to value relationships according to their longevity? Who benefits and who suffers because of this? What narratives impact people who aren't in long-term relationships, for whatever reason? What does the length of a relationship say, if anything, about the quality of the relationship, as experienced by the people in it?

• Consider people who are in open relationships, or who practice polyamory, or who engage in "serial monogamy." What are the discourses from your professional training as a therapist about people who struggle with or reject long-term monogamy?

By now, I hope that you're reflecting not only on the various discourses that shape the meanings we make of sex and sexuality but also on how this "natural" act, and the many identity categories we associate with it, is discursively produced.

From a constructionist, queer-theory perspective, sex and sexuality are culturally and historically contingent. Indeed, Tiefer (2004) points out in her book *Sex Is Not a Natural Act* that what we in contemporary North American society consider to be sexuality would be unrecognizable to people in some different cultures or from some different times. Many of the categories (or, *micro labels*) common today, such as *asexual*, *bisexual*, *pansexual*, *demisexual*, *omnisexual*, or *polyamorous*, were not a regular part of North American discourse only a few years ago.

Q-TIPS: WHAT IS SEX?: UNPACKING OUR ASSUMPTIONS ABOUT SEXUAL ACTIVITIES, BODY PARTS, AND IDENTITIES

What exactly is *sex*? When I search using the dictionary app on my computer, I get this: "(chiefly with reference to people) sexual activity, including specifically sexual intercourse."

When I search "sex" on Merriam-Webster, "SEXUAL INTERCOURSE" appears as a live link to the following definition:

1. heterosexual intercourse involving penetration of the vagina by the penis: COITUS (which is defined as: "physical union of male and female genitalia accompanied by rhythmic movements);
2. intercourse (such as anal or oral intercourse) that does not involve penetration of the vagina by the penis.

Looking at these definitions through a queered lens helps us notice the impact of normative discourses on sex, bodies, and identities.

- First, notice how *sex* is assumed to mean *intercourse*—and, still more specifically, penis-in-vagina, or PIV, sex, unless it is otherwise specified (as in the second definition). Even then, both definitions involve penetration by a penis. This discourse clearly centers heteronormativity and cisgender men's experiences. It also erases all experiences—even those of cisgender hetero men—that do not include penetration by a penis. These discourses actively shape what experiences people of all genders *should* have, and compare themselves to. PIV sex becomes the thing to achieve, the activity against which all other sexual activities are compared. Think about how this definition erases people who don't prefer (or can't have) sex in this way. Be careful not to assume (or impose) a hierarchy of sex acts that portray anyone's way of doing it as less legitimate than other ways

- Notice how the definition of intercourse itself not only privileges heterosexuality, but assumes cisness. The use of "male and female genitalia" conflates anatomy with gender identity; this is a clue that these are cis-centric definitions. Men are not the only people with penises and women are not the only people with vaginas.

What is a queered response to these definitions?

In your practice, it's important that you ask questions that invite people to (1) share how they define sex and (2) unpack how normative ideas about what qualifies as sex impact their lives

Furthermore, it's critical that you uncouple anatomy from gender—in your head and in your language. De-gendering language means being descriptive (e.g., "people with clits") and—very importantly—asking clients what language *they* use, and following their lead. This is especially critical when working with people whose bodies resist normative ideas, such as trans folks and people with disabilities.

Think back to my conversation with Logan. His experience of 3M—dominant messages of masculinity, and those about sex and sexuality perpetuated and circulated through movies and other media—exemplifies how discourse influences identity, and how one should perform any given identity. These sexual discourses impact not only the meanings people make of sex, but also their behaviors and experiences. Logan's distress and struggle to be a good partner—and, specifically, a good *sexual* partner—demonstrate just how influential sexual discourses are on people's lived experiences. Logan aspired to be an attentive partner to Crystal, but prevailing discourses caught him up in trying to meet their ostensible standards of masculinity in a heterosexual relationship.

In my conversation with Logan, we sought to identify the practices (e.g., being communicative, thoughtful, attentive, and responsible, and enhancing the relationship) that helped him live into his aspirations and intentions. These became the foundation for his preferred identity. This process involved queering masculinity, as well as sex and sexuality; subverting dominating narratives; and replacing them with counter narratives that reflected Logan and Crystal's relational ethic.

Obviously, this practice is not just for working with matters of sex and sexuality. Throughout this book we've focused on deconstructing discourses and co-constructing conversations that center people's values, hopes, and aspirations. This is central to narrative practice.

Now let's take a closer look at how queer theory uniquely approaches matters of pleasure, bodies, and desire.

From Sex Positive to Sex Critical

Queer theory offers a particularly useful methodology for deconstructing discourses around sex. *Queering* sex involves resisting essentialist notions of sex that are situated in discourse. It also means acting in opposition to the stigma and shame launched against those who dare challenge the highly policed norms of prevailing discourses.

Queering sex allows us to resist oppressive or limiting cultural narratives, and helps us to construct preferred and liberating alternatives to them.

What are some of the common discourses that are specific to sex, desire, and pleasure in 21st-century North America? What normative ideas are likely to be imposed on people's sexual practices?

In her seminal work, *Thinking Sex: Notes for a Radical Theory of the Politics of Sexuality*, anthropologist Gayle Rubin (1984) points to a sexual hierarchy that validates and privileges certain sexual practices within particular contexts and pathologizes others. Rubin coined the term *sex negativity* to describe this practice (and the discourses it generates) of conferring value on certain practices while stigmatizing others.

This binary consists of what Rubin calls *a charmed circle* and *the outer limits*. Unearned privileges are afforded to those who engage in sex within the charmed circle. This sphere of "good, normal, natural, blessed sexuality" (p. 281) includes:

- Heterosexual sex
- Sex performed within marriage
- Monogamous sex
- Procreative sex
- Noncommercial sex
- Sex in pairs
- Sex in a relationship
- Sex between members of the same generation
- Sex in private
- Sex without pornography
- Bodies only
- Vanilla sex.

Rubin identifies sexual activities that fall outside the charmed circle as "bad, abnormal, unnatural, damned sexuality." These outer-limits practices include:

- Homosexual sex
- Sex between unmarried people
- Promiscuous sex
- Non-procreative sex
- Commercial sex
- Sex alone or in groups
- Casual sex
- Cross-generational sex
- Sex in public
- Use of pornography
- Sex with manufactured objects
- Sadomasochistic sex.

When Rubin wrote this in 1984, it was groundbreaking. Today, some of it seems almost quaint. Clearly, some of the practices listed as part of the charmed circle have lost their special shine over the decades, while some located in the outer limits have achieved varying degrees of social sanction. And, of course, we can all think of some activities not listed.

An intersectional approach provides us with a more nuanced consideration of sexual practices. This approach looks at not just the practices themselves, but the people engaged in them, each of whom occupies a particular social location. For example, while unmarried sex may no longer belong in the outer limits, what about 14-year-olds engaging in unmarried sex? How is promiscuity (however it is measured) judged differently for men than for women—or for white men compared to Black men?

I encourage you to go back through the activities in both of the above lists and apply an intersectional analysis of each activity.

To be sure, what's considered in and what's considered out of line changes over time—and through the struggles of people who fight for sexual justice. And that is the point of Rubin's hierarchy: to examine the ways in which our bodies and sexual practices are constrained, judged, policed, and oppressed through discourse. Rubin compared the way that value is placed on certain sexual practices, and withheld from others, to other systems of oppression that justify the privileging of certain people and the marginalizing of others.

To resist sex negativity and the institutionalization of binaries, Rubin suggests we take a constructionist approach to sex. This means acknowledging that the human body is never unmediated by culture (i.e., discourse). Rubin's work also calls on us to evaluate sexual practices based on "the way partners treat one another, the level of mutual consideration, the presence or absence of coercion, and the quantity and quality of the pleasures they provide" (p. 283). Taking up this relational ethic would free people from the shame and stigma that often surround those who resist cultural norms.

Think back to Logan. The shame that troubled him was not so much a response to the stigma of particular practices as it was to the stigma of failing to meet the expectations of intersecting normative discourses—discourses that shaped his ideas of masculinity and a "normal" sex life. Ultimately, Logan took a stand against the idea that he should evaluate himself as a partner based on the criteria established by these discourses.

When Crystal joined us in the next session, we talked about the ways that 3M came between her and Logan. Crystal very much valued what Logan brought to their sexual relationship and, in fact, was most troubled "when I can tell he's trying to want it when he doesn't—or when he dismisses his interest in cuddling, kissing, and less explicitly sexual stuff." Over a handful of sessions, Logan and Crystal together wrote their Sexual Mission and Manifesto, in which they articulated their values and intentions for their sexual relationship. Logan also became more intentional about spending time with people (especially but not exclusively men) who challenge normative assumptions about sex and masculinity.

Sex positivity requires that we don't judge, dismiss, critique, pathologize, criminalize, or moralize about someone's sexual proclivities. It also insists that we don't try to coerce, convince, cajole, or demand that another person must participate in (or even like) something we enjoy. As sex educators Barker and Hancock (2017) point out, discrepancies in sexual preferences are inevitable, including among loving partners.

Decades have now passed since Gayle Rubin published *Thinking Sex*. It's easy to forget that her work brought about a profound shift from sex negativity to sex positivity, helping people to understand and honor the limitless differences that exist among human beings—and to liberate themselves from shame about sex. This shift has been instrumental in the struggle for sexual liberation and justice—especially for women, people with disabilities, queer and trans people, the elderly, and anyone else whose body and sexual activities are highly scrutinized.

That said, it's also important to note how—as is often true with radical revisions of oppressive systems—sex positivity has experienced a bit of mission drift in recent years. In fact, some people argue that the term *sex positivity* is now being used in ways that reproduce the same kind of sexual binaries it was meant to resist.

Critical theorist and gender and sexuality scholar Lisa Downing (2012) points out that the binary of sex negative/positive does what all binaries do: ignore complexities and render an either/or assessment. This has resulted in a kind of binary wherein sex positivity means encouraging all kinds of sexual and erotic practices in the name of sexual exploration and freedom of choice, while sex negativity means criticizing the very same practices for sexist gender representations and the promotion of sexual coercion or violence. In either case, a one-size-fits-all assessment of sexual practices, often taken out of context, prevails.

Downing acknowledges the important changes brought about by sex positivity (especially for women), but also suggests an alternative to this problematic binary: what she calls a *sex critical* stance. Taking such a stance positions us to ask critical questions of *all* forms of sexuality and all varieties of sexual practices. This matters in part because, typically, sexualities and sexual activities that are considered to be non-normative (remember the outer limits?) are the ones most likely to be questioned, while "normal" sex and sexualities tend to go uninterrogated. In addition, sex positivity has uncritically glorified all forms of sexual practices as worthy and liberatory—but it has not analyzed power relations or critiqued the ways in which some practices, in some contexts, can reinforce problematic norms (Barker, 2012).

What does this look like in people's lives? Let's return to Logan. He was very aware of the sex positive zeitgeist encouraging adventurous sex. This added to his sense that he "should" have been more adventurous in sex with Crystal. This, in turn, added to the shame that dogged him. In parallel fashion, a variety of people—queer, straight, ACE, ARO, trans, and cis—have told me that they feel judged by their partners (and sometimes by themselves) when they balk at certain sexual practices. This puts them in an impossible bind: if they say no to something they don't want to do, or that doesn't feel good to them, they may feel prudish or anti-sex—or, worse, their partner may accuse them of being that way. But the seeming alternative is to force themselves to do something that doesn't feel good, or turns them off, or hurts or disgusts them.

For example, over the last few years in my therapy practice, I've seen an increasing number of people who are in open relationships, or who are considering opening up their previously monogamous relationships. (Indeed, the conversation about open relationships has exploded in popular media, such as *The New York Times* (Dominus, 2017), *The Huffington Post* (Williams, 2017), *O Magazine* (Vincenty, 2019), *The Guardian* (Jones, 2018), *Men's Health* (Engle, 2019), and *The Atlantic* (Buder, 2018), all of which have featured stories about how to successfully navigate such relationships). Some of my clients feel that open partnerships are "more evolved" than monogamy.

That was the case with Bri and Dani, two cis queer women in their early 30s. Bri was Black and Dani was Puerto Rican. They had been together for four years, and had shared a home that they had bought together for the last two and half. In recent months, they had talked about getting married. They met with me to discuss opening their relationship.

Bri explained that she had told Dani when they first got together that she was "open-curious." Although she had never had an open relationship with a past partner, Bri had been in relationships that "had squishy boundaries—but we never really talked about it or negotiated how we wanted it to work." Bri had done a lot of research about open relationships—reading *The Ethical Slut*, attending a workshop at a local sex accessories store, and talking with friends and relatives who were in open relationships. "I really believe," she said,

> that monogamy doesn't work, and isn't realistic. It places too much emphasis on sex, while at the same time doesn't value it enough. And as a woman, I want to resist the idea of my sexuality as something someone else can own. I love our relationship, and I want to be with Dani. And I think opening the relationship is good for us.

Dani said, "This isn't usually something that comes out of my mouth, but I guess I'm more conservative than I thought." By this, she meant that the idea of an open relationship was

> really pretty out there, and just doesn't seem right to me. As a theoretical and political exercise, I understand what Bri is saying...but it just doesn't feel right, and I'm not sure it's what I want. But I love Bri and this relationship, and I'm open to talking about it.

Dani added that she hadn't had as many sexual relationships as Bri, and both women agreed that Dani's more limited experience had been an issue earlier in their relationship, because it created "a power thing." They were concerned that this issue was resurfacing with their talk of opening the relationship. Dani said, "I know I'm a bit behind the times on this."

That's a telling statement. It implies that Dani was well aware not only of Bri's interests and beliefs, but of the powerful discourse of uncritical sex positivity. She had accepted without question the notion that open relationships are somehow superior to monogamous ones. Of course, unquestioningly following the normative script of uncritical sex positively is no less problematic than uncritically abiding by the normative script of monogamy.

One of the key points of a sex critical stance is undoing principles of universality. Why should we believe that one kind of relationship is best at all times, in all contexts, for every kind of person?

I told Dani and Bri that I did not view any one particular relationship structure as better or healthier than another. But I added that being queer and practicing queered therapy didn't mean that I automatically sanctioned any and every sexual activity, especially when it is taken out of context. I told them that I was interested in helping them be intentional about their decisions, and to make those decisions based on their values and aspirations for the relationship. What kind of arrangement (monogamous, open, something in between, or something else entirely) would be best for their relationship? What would each arrangement make possible, and what possibilities would it shut down? In asking these and other, similar questions, we were able to move from a sex positive stance to a sex critical one.

Being sex critical means that no sexual practice should be free of critical questioning, particularly in regard to issues of power. Queer theory's focus on questioning power relations and exposing norms (especially about sexuality and gender) provides an apt methodology for a sex critical stance; narrative therapy offers methods to put that stance into practice. Taking a sex critical stance allows you and your clients to consider the effects and meanings of any particular sexual activity. It also allows them to contemplate whether or not it allows them to embody their values and live into their preferred identities.

Q-TIPS: WHAT'S LOVE GOT TO DO WITH IT?

One of the most powerful discourses about sex is that it goes hand-in-hand with love. There's a laundry list of beliefs surrounding this pairing. Some examples:

- Sex is best when you're in love
- You should be in love with someone before having sex with them
- Loveless sex is empty and unsatisfying
- Sexless love is a sign of a troubled relationship.

Another powerful discourse is the essentialist narrative that men want sex and women want love (or a committed relationship).

A queer theory-informed therapist who takes a sex critical stance will first engage reflexively with these ideas, in order to unpack their own assumptions and consider alternative perspectives. Then, in the therapy room, they will invite clients to explore how these narratives impact them.

Long ago, people who experience love and sexual attraction created language (and continue to create language) to speak their lives into the world. In recent years, a variety of micro-labels and micro-identities have emerged on the asexual (ACE) and aromantic (ARO) spectrum, enabling a wider range of people to speak their lives into the world. The language around gender identities and sexual orientations is constantly changing. It's crucial that therapists ask clients how *they* experience love, sex, and the relationship between the two—as well as what language they use to describe their experiences.

Teach the Children Well: Queer and Trans Youth Sexuality and You

If you think there are a lot of discourses about sex (and there are!), take a moment to consider the cultural stories about young people and sex. I don't mean sexual orientation or identity. I'm talking about *doing it*— whatever it is.

What discourses shape our ideas about youth as sexual people? About young people's pursuit of, and preferences around, pleasure? How do these discourses stay the same or change, depending on the gender of a young person? What about when we think about queer youth vs. straight youth, or white youth vs. BIPOC youth? How do those discourses change based on how a particular young person's body is racialized? What about the specific intersections of gender, sexuality, race, class, and ability where a young person may live?

And what do I mean by *youth* or *young person*? The United Nations defines *youth* as people between the ages of 15 and 24. YouthPolicy.org, an international think-tank focused on research, policy, and journalism by and for young people, defines youth as people under 25 years old, and divides them into three stages: early adolescence (under 14), middle adolescence (15–17), and late adolescence (18–24).

As therapists who work with youth, we need to reflect on our own ideas about youth sexuality—not as an identity, but in terms of individual human beings' desires, pursuit of pleasure, and sexual activity.

I'd like you to consider the following self-reflexive questions. As you do, be sure to observe how your responses may change (or stay the same) when you consider them about queer, ACE, ARO, or straight youth. Also pay attention to the impact of other markers of social location, such as gender, race, class, and ability:

• What have I been culturally and professionally trained to believe about youth and sex?
• What have been some of the specific messages about youth and sex that I have received from the media, pop culture, my culture, my religion, my professional training, my family, etc.?
• What values and relational ethic do my attitudes seem to support? Is this an ethic that I want to continue to embrace? Why or why not?
• What values and relational ethic do I want to practice? What changes might I make in order to live into my preferred ethic?

(Adapted from Tilsen, 2013)

As you critically question your practices with young people in matters of sex, pay close attention to your assumptions about, and knowledge of, queer and trans youth and their sexual interests and activities.

It's also crucial that you be ready and able to engage in nitty-gritty conversations about sex with young people. Many queer and trans youth will have few, if any, safe-enough people to have these conversations with. In fact, sex education is especially lacking for queer and trans youth. Consider the following findings:

• Fewer than 5% of queer and trans students had health classes that included positive representations of LGBT-related topics (Kosciw, Greytak, Palmer, & Boesen, 2014)

- Only 12% of young people surveyed reported that their sex education classes covered same-sex relationships (Jones & Cox, 2015)
- In a 2015 study published by Planned Parenthood, queer and trans youth reported that the sex education they received (if they received any at all) focused primarily or exclusively on heterosexual relationships between cisgender people
- The young people in this study reported having few adults to talk to about sex, and said that they mostly sought information from peers and/or online.

While we're in a cultural shift in which queer, and to a lesser extent trans, youth are gaining greater visibility and latitude in the world, one need look no further than sex ed classes and school dances[i] to see where explicit homophobia and transphobia still persist. In general, the focus on queer youth identities—bolstered by the "born this way" anthem and the assimilationist claim that "we're just like everyone else"—has helped forge a path toward greater inclusion and safety. Yet, when we get close to matters of sex, the protection of bio-essentialism and liberal-humanism wears thin. When the moral panic around youth sexuality meets with the enduring stigma of so-called "gay sex," queer and trans young people are often left in the dark, dis-belonged, and at risk.

What's a queer theory-informed narrative therapist to do?

I work extensively with queer and trans youth, so I asked them directly about this (Tilsen, 2010, 2013). What these young people told me, over and over again, is that the most important and valuable thing about my conversations with them about sex is that I showed up unfazed, without judgment or hesitation, ready to have real talk. Of course, they also expect that I have good information; that I'm up to date on current sexual trends; and that, when I don't know something, I say so, and I learn.

Queering your practice with queer and trans young people also involves respecting their agency as sexual beings and supporting their right to story their own sexual lives with dignity.

When I first met with Tay, a white 15-year-old, they described themselves as "a loud and proud nonbinary person." Tay had asked their parents for therapy because they were experiencing "a shitload of body dysphoria." Tay had quit playing soccer (a game they had loved since they were four) because they couldn't play while binding, and the dysphoria was too strong to allow them to forego binding.[2]

As we worked together—and after they joined a teen gender group—Tay was able to "keep the dysphoria to a low hum most of the time." This allowed them to start playing soccer again. This meant several things: they were doing something they loved; they got to experience competence, while feeling good in their body; and they had a sense of belonging with supportive peers.

After a few months' break from therapy, Tay returned. They told me that they had begun dating Colin, a white 15-year-old cis young man they met at debate camp. As Tay talked about Colin (who Tay said was "hot as hell"), their excitement about the relationship was palpable. Yet underlying Tay's excitement, and somewhere between the words they were speaking, I heard some hesitation and unease. There was something else Tay wanted to say, but I could tell that I needed to be the one to open the door to those words. (Often, in matters of sex, it's important to deliberately open some conversational doors for young people.) Here's where our conversation went next:

JULIE: Tay, it sounds like you really like Colin, and that you two are having a lot of fun together, and you really take care of each other…

TAY: Yeah. I wouldn't say he's my best friend, because Maddie has been my best friend since fourth grade, but he's such a good friend, not just a boyfriend. And he's never misgendered me or used my deadname. He tells people I'm his boo, and doesn't let anyone call me his girlfriend or boyfriend.

JULIE: That's how it should be, right!? So, Tay, I'm super glad you have such an awesome person in your life…I'm wondering if, along with all the awesome stuff, is there something that's making some trouble for you?

TAY (LOOKING DOWN): Well, it's kind of hard to talk about. It's sort of about dysphoria again…

JULIE: Thanks for telling me, and I'm sorry dysphoria is back causing problems. Tay, is it hard to talk about because it's complicated and you don't understand it, or you think I may not? Or, because it's hard to find words? Or, maybe, because it's embarrassing? Or am I totally off and it's something else?

TAY: No, you're not off. I guess it's some of all of it, but mostly it's just kind of embarrassing…

I asked Tay if I could I take some guesses. I said that I had some ideas about what might be happening, and I wanted them to have a chance to confirm or correct them.

Tay liked this idea and said, "I think if you start talking, I'll be able to eventually."

I asked Tay how they would let me know if we were getting into something they didn't want to talk about. (Even though I was about to put my foot on the conversational gas pedal, I wanted Tay to be in charge of putting on the brakes.) They smiled and said, "Oh, you should know me well enough by now to know that I'll give you the stink-eye."

I wondered out loud about what it meant for Tay to be dating, and what it meant to be dating a cis guy. I also asked about what sexual activities, if any, either of the young people were interested in, and how they were talking about and negotiating them. Tay listened carefully, nodding slowly at times, and answered each question thoughtfully. Then our conversation went here:

JULIE: When you said that it's sort of about dysphoria, it makes me wonder if some kind of touching has happened, or you're worried it could happen, or you're not sure how to bring it up to Colin....Like, I know this is totally a thing for non-binary folks—what parts of your body are OK to touch, or how you think about the touching and your gender identity...

TAY (INTERRUPTING ME): Yeah, that's it. All of it. I know gender isn't sexuality, but I feel like I don't know what's OK to like and not like as a non-binary person. I really like him, and I thought I'd be OK if he touched my hips, but I got all weird when he put his arm around my waist while we were walking. He could tell, so he put his arm around my shoulders, and I was afraid his hand would touch the side of my chest. It didn't, but that was all I could think about.

As we talked, I asked Tay what they knew about their body in terms of what it liked and didn't like. I asked them what they did to find out what their body likes, and if they'd like some information about useful ways to explore it. Then, with Tay's permission, I got out my phone, and together we looked at a website with information for trans and nonbinary youth about sex, dating, and masturbation. (While everyone's sexual satisfaction with partners will be improved through self-exploration, this is especially so for trans and nonbinary youth.)

Tay said, "Julie, this is way more useful sex ed than a whole semester at school."

Then I asked Tay about consent. "Well," Tay said, "that's actually something Colin is annoyingly good at." Tay explained that Colin "asks if he can do anything—hold my hand, hug me, whatever." They said that they'd learned from Colin to ask before they touch him "and pretty much everyone else in my life accept my dog."

Next, Tay talked about the importance of consent in light of dysphoria and its fickleness. Tay said, "Sometimes I do like to be touched in certain ways, but at other times dysphoria makes it hard." I told them that lots of trans and nonbinary people experience this.

Then I brought up birth control. (At first Tay was embarrassed, but then they said, "Carry on.") Our discussion about birth control and STI prevention served as an entry into a conversation about the intersection of gender identity and sexual practices. This was a component of their identity project that Tay admitted they hadn't considered much before.

We continued these conversations over several more weeks. During this time, Tay signed up to meet with a peer educator at Planned Parenthood. This provided them with extra training in sex ed and responsible relationships, and opportunities to reflect on what did and didn't suit them.

In our final meeting, Tay said to me, "I think most people have no effing clue about how complicated sex can be for trans and nonbinary people, and for teenagers generally. How could they possibly get it for trans and non-binary teens?"

Queering sex is a matter of confronting normative discourses. When addressing sex, queering involves entertaining doubt where you may have held certainties about anatomy, desire, pleasure, love, relationships, and identity. It is a practice of accountability and humility. Just like with Tay, where I encouraged them to engage in self-exploration by going solo before getting busy with a partner, therapists need to first be self-reflexive. After engaging critically with their own beliefs and assumptions, they will be better able to support their clients around matters of sex (and everything else).

Notes

1. There are numerous instances of schools prohibiting students from taking same-sex partners to dances and otherwise instituting two sets of rules for straight students and queer students at school dances.
2. Some AFAB trans people bind their chests in order to reduce body dysphoria by flattening their chests. This creates a gender presentation more in line with their identity. Because binding compresses the chest, exercising while wearing a binder can be dangerous.

7

NOT EVERYONE BELIEVES IN UNICORNS

Storying Queer Resistance to Rejection and Hate

A Say or a Relationship?

Juno grimaced as her mom talked. "I know Juno doesn't want anything to do with her dad," Molly said, "especially now that she's transitioning, but unless and until I go to court and fight for full legal custody, we don't have a choice."

I had been working with Juno and her mom for about four months. Juno was 11 years old, mixed race (Molly was Black and Curt, her father, white), and an amazing artist. She also wanted to go on puberty blockers. Molly was actively supporting Juno's transition in every way possible, including buying her girls clothes, using her chosen name and pronouns, advocating for her at school, learning about gender, and participating with Juno in a social/support group for trans youth and their families. Molly also supported Juno's desire to go on blockers. "But," Molly said, "that's a decision I literally don't have the right to make on my own."

Molly had been divorced from Curt, Juno's dad, for ten years. Both Juno and her mom described Curt as "difficult." Juno added that "he's gotten weird about religion, too, and I don't need to hear him tell me I'm an insult to God." Molly explained that the custody arrangement permitted Curt to see Juno every other weekend, some holidays, and part of Juno's summer break. Because Curt lived two hours away from Molly and their children,

Juno didn't spend all the time with him that their custody arrangement allowed. "In reality," Molly said, "Curt has never been very involved with Juno, or with her older brother."

The problem was that Juno's clinic, and her gender doctor, required authorization from both custodial parents before prescribing blockers. Molly said that Curt was interested in attending a therapy session. She said that he had "made himself crystal clear about his opposition to transition, and in particular any medical interventions. He won't listen to me. I'm hoping he'll hear it from you, the professional."

We scheduled a time for Molly and Curt to come in together. Juno didn't want anything to do with it, and Molly and I didn't want to subject her to any extra pain and stress.

Molly and Juno had shared with me many times how Curt was simply not around for Juno or her older brother, Kyle, who was 15. They didn't have any hope or reason to think that he would change. While I believed them, I also believed that it was my responsibility to provide Curt with every possible opportunity to show up for Juno and be a supportive dad.

I hadn't ruled out going all "Dr. Tilsen" on him, and laying out the stats about the risk factors for unsupported trans youth—but that was not where I was going to start. As a narrative therapist, I understood that Curt, like everyone else, was subject to the prevailing discourses about gender. I wasn't going to participate in the burden of individualism by thinking that he's a bad person or parent; I was committed to understanding Curt in context.

I began the conversation by inviting Molly and Curt to speak to their missions as parents (as I described in Chapter 5). This took them both off guard a bit, as it obliged them to witness each other as they each talked about wanting their child to be happy and healthy. It was also, quite possibly, the first time they hadn't been at each other's throat for a long time. I knew that Molly wanted me to give Curt a good talking to, and that Curt expected to be lectured by the big, bad queer therapist. I was earnest in my efforts to understand Curt and create space for him.

Throughout the conversation, Curt dead-named and misgendered Juno. Each time, Molly corrected him under her breath. I asked Curt about his faith and how it informed his parenting. He said that he's "grateful to God for the opportunity to be a parent." I asked him, "Given the significance of your faith in your life, how would you say it guides your decisions as a dad?"

He said that he hadn't had many opportunities to parent his children very closely recently. I asked him—eventually, multiple times—to say more about this. Each time, his response was vague, and I watched through the corner of my eye as Molly become more and more exasperated.

Soon I understood that, for a long time, Curt had been comfortable with intermittent contact with Juno and little parental responsibility—until the matter of medical transition came up. I still wasn't giving up on him, but I wasn't going to let him off the hook. I wanted to find a way to invite him to responsibility (Jenkins, 1990).

I asked Curt some more questions about the role of religion in his life. Curt talked freely. He said that "God doesn't make mistakes," and that "you're either male or female, like God made you, and you stay that way from birth." He added that, "mutilating your body is an insult to God." I recalled Juno's words.

Curt also said, "Cam (Juno's dead name) is just going through a phase." I could tell that he was upset, even scared. I asked him, "Curt, do you feel like you have to choose between your God and your child?"

He became tearful and nodded his head. "Yes, yes I do. And that hurts."

I told him, "I can't imagine how painful that would be."

Briefly, he looked me in the eyes and nodded his head once.

"Curt," I asked, "do you think God would make the mistake of expecting a parent to have to make that kind of decision? To choose his faith or choose his child?"

Curt choked back tears and sat up straight. He answered a question I had not asked: "Cam will be 18 pretty soon. I only have a say until he's 18. He can do what he wants then. But until then, there will be a different path we take."

I paused and took a sip of my coffee. Then I leaned toward him and asked softly, "Curt, do you want to have a say, or do you want to have a relationship?"

Molly started crying.

Curt stared blankly at me. He asked me what I meant.

I told him that I was confused because, up until he made his comment about only having a say until Juno is 18, I had understood that he was longing for a relationship with Juno. "When you have a relationship with someone, you have a say in their life...but having a say doesn't mean you have a relationship."

Molly nodded her head vigorously.

I said, "When I have a relationship with someone, whether it's my partner, or my friend, or a student, or a client, I do have a say in their life. But if I can only show up with whatever kind of authority I may have and demand to have a say, it's likely that I don't have a relationship."

Curt said nothing, but his tears came back. I waited. "I want a relationship," he said.

I told him that I believed him, but that my guess was that he thought a relationship wasn't possible. He wanted a relationship, but felt he would have to settle for a say.

Curt sighed and nodded his head.

I told him I wanted to ask a hard question. I told him that he didn't need to answer in front of Molly and me if he didn't want to, but that I hoped he'd give me his permission to ask, so that he could think about it. He agreed.

I said, "Curt, in your heart of hearts, and before your God, if you could imagine away the issue around gender and identity, would you say that your relationship with Juno is one that would afford you the kind of say you want to have? Or have there been other problems that have kept you from having the kind of relationship that gives you a say?"

Curt fidgeted slightly. "Well, it's hard because of the distance…"

I knew that he was referring to the 100 miles of highways between his house and Molly's, but I said, "Yeah, there's really a big gulf between you and Juno. No wonder you felt you had to grasp for parental authority rather than lean into the relationship. Curt, would you be willing to think about how your faith might guide you to bridge that gulf?"

Curt said that he would.

We were near the end of the hour, and both parents agreed to meet again. We scheduled a time during the upcoming week that worked for Curt to make the trip to Minneapolis.

Three days later, Molly called to tell me that she and Juno would be coming to that appointment, not Curt. Curt "had a change of heart after talking with his pastor." Molly was reading from an email he sent her. He now was agreeing to meet with Molly in mediation to re-visit the custodial arrangements. "Apparently," Molly said, "he's chosen his God, not his child."

Not everyone believes in unicorns.

After my session with Molly and Curt, at first I was cautiously hopeful. Over the years, I've had many conversations with parents caught in the same agonizing crucible of irreconcilability that Curt found himself in. Some come out of it tempered by the struggle, softened in hard spots, and freed to envision a bond with religion and God that allows them to be in relationship with their queer or trans child. These parents craft new stories for themselves, their faith, their children, and the relationships among them all. What these stories are and what they come to mean for the people involved can vary, but shifts do happen. The common element for parents who go in refusing to accept their child's identity and come out open to it is this: a newfound willingness to step into complexities and entertain doubt about their own certainties.

Other parents, like Curt, exit the crucible before tempering occurs, steeled by the conflict of values, clinging to authoritative stories of certitude, told over and over again. They submit to the same kind of power that they try to impose on their queer and trans children—a power that that they won't allow to be questioned. In a world storied in this way, complexities and uncertainties are fictions because everything is set and clear. Asking questions is above one's station.

I never doubted that Curt believed that he loved Juno; his pain was a testimony to this belief. But I say "belief" here because, as bell hooks (2001) observes, love for another person requires that we fully accept them and don't inflict harm on them.

I genuinely felt sad for Curt. I understood that he was influenced by discourses that shaped and limited how he felt about and responded to Juno. These discourses involved gender, of course, but they also involved young people's agency, their right of self-determination, and the role of parental (and, especially, fatherly) authority. (Note here how queer theory and narrative therapy informed how I positioned myself with Curt, as well as how I viewed him as situated in the discursive world.)

I reflected on our session and talked with a colleague about it. What could I have done differently? I'm not arrogant enough to believe that I can connect with and make a difference for everyone; but I believe that, for each client, someone and something can make a difference. My colleague offered a suggestion, and I agreed that it was worth trying.

I asked Molly if she and Juno would be OK if I sent Curt a letter. I wanted to invite his feedback about our session and see if I could account for anything that had landed wrong for him. I wanted to keep the door open and the conversation going.

Molly appreciated the idea and my request, but she did not want me to contact Curt. "You know him better than I do," I told her.

Not everybody believes in unicorns.

What do we do when important people in our clients' lives attack their dignity, humanity, and very way of being in the world? How do we stand with queer and trans people, and others who resist normativity, when they're faced with stigma, hostility, state-sponsored inequities, or economic, spiritual, sexual, or physical violence? How do we partner with people to construct stories that resist the stories that cast them out as sinners, criminals, or sick people?

This chapter addresses how to use queer theory-informed narrative therapy to attend to these concerns. In particular, I introduce practices that not only validate people's experience of injustice and oppression, but also bring forward their agency and dignity.

De-Privatizing Your Practice: Fostering Belonging in the Age of Disconnection

While my interactions with Curt came to an abrupt end, my work with Juno and Molly continued. Molly took steps to clear a legal path that authorized her to consent to blockers for Juno. I continued to support Juno and Molly throughout transition, especially as Juno navigated the capriciousness of middle school. I could see that Juno was going to be OK regardless of Curt; as Molly and Juno pointed out, Curt had left both of them a long time ago.

What helped Juno be in a good place was everything she and Molly had been doing long before Curt began questioning her transition. In addition to coming to therapy, Juno and Molly *got connected*. Juno participated in social groups for trans youth and in the GSA at her school. Molly reached out to parents with trans children. Together, they connected with trans youth and their families through social media, and they participated in social, supportive, and political activities where their identities (Juno's as a trans girl and Molly as a supportive parent of a trans girl) were seen and valued. They became part of a community. They never had to go it alone. They went from an experience of dis-belonging to one of belonging.

As we've seen in the first three chapters of this book, two of the most powerful normative discourses that burden queer and trans people are baked into conventional psychotherapy: individualism and neoliberalism. To counter this, much of my focus with queer and trans people often involves de-privatizing my practice, in order to resist the burden of individualism and help them feel belonged.

What do I mean by de-privatizing my practice? Let's take a look.

I often ask clients, "What will be different when you no longer need to come see me?" In response, people have told me, too many times to count, some version of "I won't feel so alone." The last thing I want to do in response to the dis-belonging and isolation of marginalization is to offer *only* conversations behind a closed door in a private setting—that is, traditional psychotherapy. That would further privatize social problems, locating the problem in individual persons—*and* putting the burden of the fix there as well.

As a therapist, my role is to help support queer and trans people—and other transgressors of norms (recall Logan from Chapter 6)—in constructing new and preferred stories, and in reclaiming their lives from familial, societal, and state rejection and violence. This requires a different landscape, and a different cast of characters, from narratives that are hurtful or hopeless. Our identities are forged in relationships; new stories require new relationships. My role is partly as a facilitator of these connections.

What does this involve? Here are several ways that I—and you—can help to foster belonging and widen people's worlds:

Encourage clients to participate in therapeutic, social, political, educational, or support groups. It's important to stay current on what's available in your area for queer and trans people and their family members. I encourage you to do the same for people in polyamorous, open, or BDSM/kink relationships. (Sex shops often offer workshops or classes for these folks.)

In addition to therapy groups that focus on queer and trans identities and/or related issues, there are groups that offer social opportunities and peer support. Also, many of my clients have found belonging and purpose in getting politically involved with queer and trans issues—for example, by volunteering for issue-related campaigns, supporting political candidates, etc.

Of course, individual needs and preferences matter, as does the timing of someone's participation in a group. Having said that, I find that many people start with therapy because that's a known path to receiving support. Yet what really makes a difference for many people is *being in community with other people like them*. I've had queer and trans clients who join queer softball teams, online D&D groups, or knitting clubs, where they experience the belonging that sets them on their way. (This is not meant in any way to minimize any trauma or other significant struggles that bring people to therapy. I'm simply suggesting that not all support need to be professional and formal.)

Encourage clients to connect with other people through social media and online communities. For some people, opportunities for connecting in person with others are very limited. Learn about and recommend online communities that bring queer and trans connections to people all over the country or world. For many folks, meeting online is a safe-enough first step, especially if they are concerned about their physical safety, or if anxiety is a barrier to meeting others in person.

Some of the trans youth I work with who live in rural areas participate in an online chat group for trans youth. Many parents I know have found support and belonging through Facebook groups organized by and for parents of queer and trans children.

Connect clients with people in the community. Connecting clients to other people, rather than making a referral to another professional, may seem unconventional. But for narrative therapists, it is not. We often connect clients with others who have similar experiences. Indeed, this is central to de-privatizing therapy. I connect parents with parents; young queer and trans people with older queer and trans people; and all kinds of people with cultural leaders, elders, and clergy who support queer and trans people. I ask clients and former clients, as well as friends and colleagues, to make themselves available—and for their suggestions.

For example, I often ask adult trans folks if they'll meet with young adults who are early in transition and don't know many trans people. I frequently put parents of queer and trans kids in touch with other parents. I connect couples who are new to (or considering) opening their relationships to couples who have. I of course only facilitate connections that people are interested in exploring—and I always ask for their consent in advance.

Invite meaningful others to sessions. For some people, meeting others online, in the community, or even at a structured event might be too big of a leap at first. They may prefer inviting people to our sessions, where I can be there to facilitate connections. This may involve inviting significant people in someone's life (friends, family members, mentors, teachers, etc.). Or it may mean bringing in people I know or have access to (such as the parents of queer and trans children, or an elder or religious leader), to begin a supportive relationship with a client.

Read, listen to, and watch the personal accounts of other people. The unicorn lives on YouTube. Many queer and trans people first learn what is possible through the online presence of other queer and trans people. This is where many people first begin to see a future for themselves. This is especially true of YouTube, where people share their coming out stories, experiences with therapists and medical providers, advice for transition, and general encouragement and support. Queer and trans people (especially young people) can also find their way to the social media accounts of others like them, who can help them make meaning of their own experience.

Sometimes, I'll take some time in session to watch or read some of these accounts with my clients. This provides them with an opportunity to consider what stories they hear, and to unpack their impact and the meanings that people make of them. Together, my client and I then imagine what they might include in a future account of their lived experience. As we explore this, I might ask them what they hope their sharing would make possible for others, and what doing so would say about where they are in their own journey.

Facilitate a letter-writing campaign. Letter-writing campaigns are another narrative therapy practice that connects clients with appreciative and meaningful friends and family members and the stories those people carry about them. The purpose of letter-writing campaigns is to help people re-member their lives (Hedtke & Winslade, 2005; Madigan, 2011) with aspects of themselves that have been taken over by problems— and to do so with the stories of their preferred identities that supportive people in their lives carry. Letter-writing campaigns help to de-privatize therapy, and they foster belonging by inviting other people (and their perspectives) into the conversation.[1]

For example, David, a 55-year-old white gay man, chose to do a letter-writing campaign when he ended an abusive relationship that had left him full of self-doubt and anxiety. Together, David and I crafted a letter that invited significant people of his choosing (a sample invitation letter is in the appendix) to then write letters to David in which they would share their memories and experiences of him as competent, compassionate, and talented. David and I read the letters in our sessions and David re-claimed aspects of his identity, including skills and knowledges, that others had carried for him in their stories.

All of the practices above are meant to cultivate connections and belonging, especially for queer and trans people (and their family members) who experience isolation and dis-belonging.

Helping people connect to worlds where they are seen and valued is imperative. In affirming communities and supportive relationships, we all can take a stand against the oppressive and de-humanizing stories constructed within the narrow worlds of fear and hate.

Diagnosing Discourses

In Chapter 3, I discussed the narrative therapy practice of externalizing and situating problems in discourse. An extension of this practice, *diagnosing discourses* (Tilsen, 2013), can be useful in resisting the burden of individualism and standing up to oppression.

Diagnosing discourses solidly locates problems in the social world and positions people to take a bird's-eye view of how their personal stories are situated within broader cultural narratives. Consider the following vignette:

Lauren, a cisgender white woman who lived in an outer suburb of a large city, was 43 when she came out as bisexual. Initially, she felt relief. She had been unhappily married for 20 years to Thad, a man who, Lauren said, "really never thought much of me."

Several months after their divorce had finalized, Lauren "scratched an itch I'd had forever" and dated a few women. Lauren's relief turned into joy as she felt she was really connecting with other people for the first time in years.

Then Thad discovered that she was seeing a woman, outed her to her conservative Catholic family of origin, and pitted her kids against her. This sent Lauren spiraling down into self-hate. She deliberately overdosed on over-the-counter pain pills.

After she was medically stabilized, she spent several days in the psychiatric unit, followed by a week of intensive day treatment.

After her treatment, she came to see me, with her gay cousin Philip, who had put her in contact with me.

Philip said that he was concerned about the therapy she received in the hospital programs "because they didn't say anything about the fucked-up world, and only tried to get her to think positive thoughts. I told her she needed a proper queer therapist."

Lauren said that she trusted Philip; that's why she had agreed to come, even though she believed, as she told me, "It's my fault for giving up and letting everything get to me. I was weak." Then she told me that suicide was "selfish, short-sighted, and cowardly."

I turned to Philip and asked him to say more about what concerned him about the therapy Lauren had received in the hospital—and what he thought might be more helpful.

PHILIP: I'm no therapist, but I've been to therapy. I think it's malpractice for the therapists there to ignore homophobia when a bisexual woman gets depressed and tries to kill herself because she got outed to a family of religious zealots.

JULIE: What part do you think Homophobia plays when Depression takes over gay or bi folks and gets them to try to kill themselves? What part do you think it's played in Lauren's life?

PHILIP: I think it has tons to do with it. I've had too many friends go that route when they've been disowned or harassed. I mean, Lauren would never do that on her own. Parts of the world, certain people in the world, hate gay people. People don't hate themselves without encouragement.

JULIE: So, you think that Homophobia encouraged Lauren to hate herself?

PHILIP: Totally. She didn't before. I know that she hated some parts of her life, being married to Thad and all, but she didn't hate herself. And she loves being a mom, and Thad and her parents are taking that from her.

JULIE: What part do you think Homophobia plays in how Thad and Lauren's parents are responding? In how the kids are balking at spending time with her?

PHILIP: Yeah, that's homophobia. Three generations of it.

JULIE: So they're all under its influence, too?

PHILIP: Yup. Completely blinded by it.

JULIE: Philip, if you think it was malpractice not to talk about Homophobia, what are your ideas about good therapy practice?

PHILIP: Well, I just don't think the depression and overdose should be taken as Lauren's bad choice and all her fault without acknowledging what's going on. I don't believe she wants to kill herself. Like I said, she wouldn't do that on her own if something wasn't pushing her.

JULIE: Philip, do you think part of the malpractice was that they diagnosed this as a suicide attempt—but it was really an attempted murder?

PHILIP: I….wait, what?

LAUREN: Yeah, you lost me, too!

JULIE: I'm thinking about what you said, Philip, and wondering if Homophobia attempted to murder Lauren? And that the malpractice was, in part, misdiagnosing this as suicide…

Q-TIPS: RE-THINKING THE DISCOURSE OF *FAMILY*

What comes to mind when you think about family? What stories, images, and feelings emerge for you?

We talk a great deal about the centrality of families, family values, and how "blood is thicker than water" (which implicates a discourse that privileges birth families over adoptive families). Sports teams and work teams talk of "being a family." Rhetorically, we ask questions such as, *How would you treat a family member?*

We tend to idealize families and see them as *inherently* good. We enshrine the word *family*—imbued with that idealized purity—above any other description or metaphor for meaningful connection.

All too frequently, though, this is not how many people experience family. It's especially not true for queer and trans people whose families of origin may have been places of pain, dis-belonging, or even violence (whether physical, sexual, psychological, emotional, or spiritual).

As therapists, it's important for us to reflect on and unpack our assumptions about family. It's also important that we ask clients *whom* the important people are in *their* lives; what those people and relationships contribute to their lives; and how they language those relationships. For example, many queer and trans people refer to their most intimate relationships as *chosen family* or *found family*.

Finally, we need to de-center white, Western understandings of family that prioritize so-called "immediate family" (i.e., parents, siblings, spouses, and children) and "blood relatives." Allow room for the varied ways in which people, cultures, and sub-cultures may constitute family.

In this book, we've looked at many different ways in which situating problems in discourse is a radical act of resisting the burden of individualism and the privatization of social problems. Nowhere is this more apparent than when we resist the individual pathology of suicide and name the discursive and institutional forces of oppression as the malefactor.

Suicide is typically conceptualized as an individual act, a choice—and, as Lauren described it, a selfish and cowardly one. White and Morris (2019) argue that conventional understandings of suicide (i.e., the prevailing discourses about it) are steeped in a biomedical model that stresses individual psychopathology and ignores (and often erases) cultural factors. This conceptualization leads to responses based on control and surveillance—which are exactly what Lauren experienced in the hospital.

Of course, shifting the problem from the individual to oppressive discourses didn't automatically change the hopelessness and despair that had engulfed Lauren. She had been painfully dis-belonged from her family and children, so she still felt as if her world had imploded around her.

However, making this shift changed the nature of our conversation—and the conversation Lauren had with herself—as well as the focus of therapy. I was able to invite Lauren to consider how she wanted to respond to Homophobia and its deadly effects. She identified how homophobia had long held sway in her life, as she noted that she had never acted on her interest in dating women because Homophobia had taught her it was wrong, and people would judge her. This helped Lauren see how, as she put it, "homophobia has planted deep roots in me, and I'm all twisted up in it now." Instead of fighting with herself by trying to shed the identity of selfish coward, Lauren could work to untangle herself from the roots of Homophobia.

Queer theory compels us to question norms, including those that uphold particular understandings of problems. These understandings include where problems are located, what causes them, and how to respond to them. When we understand that anti-queer rejection and hate are problems *constructed within particular discourses*, we must then seek responses to them that reflect this understanding.

Furthermore, queering responses to problems means disrupting expectations and norms, in order to allow the emergence of new possibilities (Tilsen, 2013). Thus, for example, recasting Lauren's suicide as murder queered how we understand the problem, and the possible ways to attend to it.

Narrative therapy practices (double listening, attending to what is absent but implicit, asking generative questions, etc.) queer the typical clinical conversation about suicide. This queering facilitates a shift from client responsibility and a focus on suicide prevention at any cost (White & Morris, 2019) to a conversation that brings forward client agency, leverages appreciative and meaningful relationships, and inspires hope and possibility.

For example, once Lauren considered the reach of Homophobia in her life, she started seeing the idea of killing herself as, in her words, "homophobia's ultimate intention." This allowed her to pivot from struggling with suicidal ideas to, as she said, "fighting for my life against a hostile force."

To help to further expand Lauren's perspective of this fight, and to generate life-giving stories, I asked her some of the following questions:

- What intentions, plans, or hopes that you've held for your life does Homophobia's ultimate intention get you to forget about?
- What do these intentions, plans, and hopes say about what matters to you—and about *who* matters to you? What kind of life would these intentions, plans, and hopes make possible?
- Who else knows you and can attest to what these intentions, plans, and hopes say about the kind of life you've been seeking to live? What stories might they share about how you've brought these ideas to life?
- How might suicidal thoughts be a protest against living a life dictated by Homophobia, in which you're regularly blocked from living into your intentions, plans, and hopes?
- When you reflect on the future you've imagined, is it one worthy of the death penalty, or one deserving to come to life?

Conversations driven by questions such as these steer clients and therapists away from formulaic assessments of suicide plans, and toward hope-full, value-based statements of plans for living. They avoid the reproduction of individualistic accounts of psychopathology. And they encourage people to re-member their lives with their personal values, as well as with people who are important to them.

When people are grappling with the pain of rejection or oppression-induced distress and trauma, they can easily live into a narrative that centers depression, self-hate, and hopelessness. As a therapist, you can help them to, instead, tap into their own values, identify their resources (including appreciative and meaningful others), and highlight their personal agency. They can then begin the project of authoring a counter narrative.

Take some time with the vignettes below and consider what discourses are diagnosable:

- Tori, a 27-year-old cisgender white woman, says her friends think there's something wrong with her because she's never been interested in sex. She enjoys meaningful and loving friendships and has a boyfriend she loves. Tori's therapist suggests that she is missing out on something necessary to being a "complete person," and believes that her lack of interest is due to some significant problems, perhaps repressed trauma. The therapist diagnoses Tori with Female Sexual Interest/Arousal Disorder (APA, 2013). What discourse(s) might you diagnose instead of diagnosing Tori?

• After their nine-year-old son, Jamari, reported being bullied in his class because he has lesbian moms, Ayanna and Vanessa, both Black and cisgender, become concerned about his safety. They check in with the school frequently and insist on chaperoning Jamari's field trips. They have become more cautious, prohibiting Jamari from going to his classmates' homes after school. School personnel claim that they have "intervened with the bullies" and that Ayanna and Vanessa are "fostering dependence by helicoptering" in Jamari's life. What discourse(s) might you diagnose instead diagnosing Vanessa and Ayanna?

• Faith is a white 33-year-old trans woman. She recently took a new job, which included health insurance that would cover vaginoplasty. She has always been somewhat ambivalent about this procedure. Faith has an active and enjoyable sex life that, as she says, "relies on my current equipment." Several of her trans women friends assumed that she would seek surgery once she had health insurance benefits that covered it. Her friends were surprised, and even judgmental, when Faith told them she really didn't want to. Her brother and sisters (all cis) were surprised, too, and told her that the surgery would "solidify" her identity as a woman. Faith assured them that her identity was "solid enough." Yet she finds herself second-guessing herself and wondering if there's something "really wrong with me" because she doesn't want to have surgery. What discourse(s) might you diagnose instead of diagnosing Faith?

Diagnosing discourses is consistent with narrative therapy's focus on situating problems in context. It helps position people to respond to limiting discourses in ways that reveal what matters to them, and what highlights their abilities and knowledges. (Note how all of these are often ignored, misread, or made invisible by conventional discourses of psychopathology and individualism.)

Response-Based Practice: Constructing the Story of Queer Resistance

"*Where there is power there is resistance*" (Foucault, 1978, p. 95). Foucault's observation about power relations has become a sort of mantra for both queer theorists and narrative therapists. People are always responding to power (including but not limited to oppressive or traumatic events) through, in Foucault's words, "a plurality of resistances, each of them a special case" (p. 96). This insight sits at the heart of *response-based practice* (Coates & Wade, 2007; Richardson, 2015; Wade, 1997; M. White, 2007), which is a powerful way to story resistance to violence and oppression.

Canadian family therapists and researchers Allan Wade and Linda Coates developed response-based practice as an alternative therapeutic approach for supporting people who have been victims of violence. Central to this approach is a shift from the language of *effects* to the language of *response*. Wades and Coates demonstrated that conventional language practices highlight *what happens to people* (i.e., the effects on them), positioning them as passive, non-agentic victims of violence or oppression.

All too often, we therapists ask effects questions that bring forward *what happens to* people, rather than *what people do* in response to what has happened to them. For example, *How bad is the dysphoria today?*, or *How do you feel about your teacher outing you to your coach?*, or *Why are you angry when your family ignores your partner?*

Effects questions aren't explicitly wrong; indeed, they help therapists to clarify important details and communicate our interest and compassion. The problem arises when we overuse them—and fail to *also* ask response-based questions.

Focusing only on effects ignores context, and tends to render systemic oppression invisible. Effects questions can generate totalizing accounts and single stories of passive victims, erasing people's agency and acts of resistance. In fact, effects language often collapses an act of violence or oppression *onto* the client's identity by obscuring the person, discourse, and/or system that did the actual harm. Below is an example of how this typically happens, in a sequence that can take place very quickly (and invisibly) in a therapy room:

Emma gay-bashed Diego.
Diego was gay-bashed by Emma.

Diego was gay-bashed.
Diego is a victim of gay-bashing.

You can see how Emma disappears from this story, while Diego's identity is reduced to victimhood. This promotes a conversation based on an inquiry into the effects of Diego's experience of fear, shame, anger, or hopelessness.

What is missing from this kind of conversation is an assumption of, and curiosity about, Diego's agency. That is, an effects-only conversation would fail to explore what actions Diego took in response to the abuse, and the meaning Diego made of his actions. It also disappears context and discourse—the systems of violence or oppression within which this interaction occurred.

Response-based practice asserts (as does Foucault) that people always respond to traumatic and oppressive experiences. These responses reveal active, agentic individuals standing up for and expressing what matters to them.

Fundamental to response-based practice is a recognition that even so-called "negative emotions" such as fear, shame, sadness, or anger are meaningful responses that reflect what matters to a person (recall my discussion of the absent but implicit in Chapter 3). As therapists, we can make the mistake of assuming that effects such as fear, shame, sadness, etc., represent only the negative results of oppression or trauma, rather than also a person's values, ethics, and intentions. Through response-based practices, and attention to the absent but implicit, we can avoid this mistake and facilitate the following shifts in language:

- From victim to agent
- From effects to response
- From a single story (usually of victimhood) to multiple stories
- From professional knowledge to local or cultural knowledges (i.e., who gets to create and tell the story—or, as we narrative therapists say, story-telling rights)
- From an individual to a relational and/or contextual frame.

(Tilsen, 2018)

Queer and trans people, like all of us, exist in a social world impacted by dominating discourses and institutions imbued with power and authority. We can queer our therapeutic practices by naming the power relations within social structures and practices, and shepherding people's stories of resistance out of the margins.

Diagnosing discourses and using response-based practice not only help us do this queering; they also center an ethic of care and relational responsibility by resisting the privatization of social problems.

Q-TIPS: FROM EFFECTS TO RESPONSE

Below are some examples of taking typical effects questions and shifting them to response-based questions.

As you consider these questions, notice how each question positions people in the story. Then ask yourself how you would describe the kind of conversation—where it's likely to go—generated by effects questions vs. response-based questions.

Effects-based	Response-based
What happened next?	What did you do?
Why did you shut down?	What skills did you use to control your feelings?
What makes you so angry?	What is anger a protest against?
How long were you checked out?	How did you know it was safe enough for you to come back?
Who else got picked on?	What did you do to take care of your friends?
How is this affecting you now?	How are you taking care of yourself now?

(Tilsen, 2018)

Queer Stories Are Stories of Resistance

Storying queer resistance requires our action on multiple fronts: de-privatizing therapy, in order to invite multiple perspectives and foster belonging; diagnosing discourses, as a refutation of the burden of individualism; and using response-based practices, as a way to re-center people as active agents in their own stories.

Partnering with people in the construction and circulation of these resistance stories also requires that we enthusiastically occupy and embrace the position of co-conspirators. We actively support queer and trans individuals, families, and communities in their reclamation of their story-telling rights (Denborough, 2014), and the dignity that comes with those rights.

Long before queer theory became an academic discipline and narrative therapy became a recognized therapeutic approach, communities of queer and trans people resisted discourses of normativity, and the institutionalization of the oppression that these discourses enabled. These acts of resistance—whether executed on a large scale and documented in history books, or carried out defiantly, yet cautiously, by individuals— serve as evidence of a long history of queer resistance. As we witness our clients' stories of resistance, we have the opportunity to connect their current stories to those of the past. This illuminates another kind of belonging for queer and trans people: the belonging to a legacy of protest, resistance, and hope—a legacy that asserts this undeniable truth: *Our existence is resistance.*

Note

1.   For more on letter-writing campaigns, see Bjoroy, Madigan, and Nylund (2015).

8

WELCOME TO QUEERTOPIA

Be the Unicorn You Want to See in the World

Mic[1] shuffled their feet as they made their way from the waiting room to my office, head down, concentrating on their phone. Tara and Jackson, Mic's mom and dad, followed.

After everyone sat down and Mic tucked away their phone, Mic sighed and said to me, "Remember when we talked about what would happen if the gender unicorn came and made all the stupid gender rules and stuff go away?"

"Yup, I do," I said. "What's got you thinking about that?"

"Well, I was just thinking it would be cool if that would happen. I mean, the gender stuff changing. Not the unicorn, necessarily."

"Yeah, it'd be cool," I said.

Mic had recently been feeling more confident and supported in their queerness. Along with other students from their school, Mic had co-led a workshop on gender non-binary identities at a queer youth conference. Mic had told me, "I made my principal read books about what non-binary is. Now she gets it." But today, Mic looked sadder than I had seen them look in a while.

"Mic," I said, "you seem super bummed out. Can you tell me a little bit about what's going on?"

With some help from Tara and Jackson, Mic told the story of a painful experience at school, in which some students made transphobic comments and intentionally mis-gendered Mic. Mic explained that the students made a point of telling their class that "President Trump doesn't think trans people are OK." This occurred during a classroom discussion of current events centered on so-called "bathroom bills.[2]"

"It's like I'm doing pretty good myself," Mic said, "but I got really down thinking about how many people are against us. I mean, trying to keep people from going to the bathroom is just mean and transphobic."

I asked, "Has thinking about the people who are against you got you forgetting about the people who are for you?"

"Not really. I mean, I know people support me….I'm thinking about other trans or non-binary kids who don't have people for them. It makes me really sad. And I'm mad, too, because it's not right."

I watched tears well up in Tara's eyes. Jackson put his arm around Mic, who leaned into him.

I was touched, too. "Mic, is that kind of a new thing for you, thinking about other trans and non-binary kids, or have you been thinking about them for a while?"

"Kinda both, but mostly new. I feel like, since I came out and I'm able to be myself, and since people support me, I should help others." Now tears welled up in Mic's eyes, too.

"So, you're saying that, now that you feel supported, you want to help other trans kids feel supported, too?"

Mic nodded as tears rolled down their face.

"Do you have some ideas about what you want to do to help?"

"That's the thing….It seems impossible, and that's why I'm depressed about it. I want to stick up for others, but…" Mic's words trailed off into a cloud of uncertainty.

I asked, "I'm wondering who's inspired you, or taught you that sticking up for others is a thing to do?"

Mic laughed, wiped their face, and said, "Um, have you even met my parents?"

We all laughed. Tara was a labor organizer and Jackson was a public defender. Mic had told me stories in previous conversations about "how they never stop talking about having to think past ourselves and to speak out if something isn't right."

"You know, Mic," Tara said, "it may be true that Dad and I have taught you to stick up for others, but you have a big heart. That's yours, the way you feel deeply for others." Jackson nodded in agreement as he gave Mic a squeeze.

Mic nodded. "I know, but what good is a big heart if I can't do anything besides yell at bullies? It doesn't change anything." Then they returned to their story from the class discussion. Mic said that they spoke up in response to the comment that President Trump didn't think trans people were OK. "I told them, 'Trump lost the popular vote, so most people don't think he's OK'!" Mic said that it felt good at the time to speak up. But they wondered what actual good it did. They said that they didn't have any ideas about what else to do about the problems for trans kids.

I asked Mic if I could ask their parents some questions. They agreed.

I asked Jackson and Tara—two people with experience as organizers and activists— what ideas they had about how to sustain hope and act in the face of systemic injustice. We had a somewhat philosophical conversation about sticking to your principles and doing the right thing—even if it doesn't seem to change things—because it says something about what matters to you. Then I asked them about specific examples of taking action on their principles.

"Well, you know," Tara said, "we've told Mic that there's an event this weekend to show support for trans people. Jackson and I are planning on going..."

Mic interrupted, "I know, I know...but what's it going to CHANGE?"

I asked, "You mean the one this Sunday on Lake Street? Yeah, I'm going, along with a whole crew of people."

Mic's eyes grew wide. "You ARE?"

"Yeah, it's in my calendar. And I've got a group of friends I'm going with. Mic, do you have some concerns about the action, like reasons why it's not a good idea?"

"I don't know....I guess I don't have a really good reason not to..." I could tell that Mic was thinking.

Jackson said to Mic, "I know you've been feeling really mad, and like standing on the street with signs in Minneapolis isn't going to help trans kids in North Carolina go to the bathroom....I think you don't want to do anything that's like a token, something meaningless." Mic nodded.

"Your mom and I respect that," Jackson said. "If it doesn't have meaning for you, it's OK; we'd never make you go. It was just an idea, something happening that we can do."

Mic looked at me and asked, "How come you're going?"

The upcoming action would involve people lining up on the sidewalks along both sides of one of Minneapolis' busiest and longest streets. Most of us would carry signs of support for transgender people. We would wave at cars and try to get people to wave back and honk their horns in solidarity (or at least approval). I told Mic that this would be a way for trans people and their accomplices to take up space, exercise their collective voice, and not allow haters to silence them or force them to stay hidden at home. Then I asked them to imagine people crammed on the sidewalk along a busy street for five miles, holding signs with supportive messages, many of them wearing rainbow-y clothes, and creating a super-queer, trans-welcoming vibe.

Mic laughed. *"You make it sound like the gender unicorn will be there, and that it'll all be perfect."*

"Ha!" I said. *"So, when you think about that, it gets you thinking about the Queertopia you imagined the unicorn would bring?"*

"Yeah! Like, everyone can be who they are without being judged. And then, when other people see that, like, even on social media, if a trans kid in North Carolina, or wherever, sees pictures, they may not feel so alone, knowing people are sticking up for them in Minneapolis. Then maybe they'll do something, and other people will see that, and do something, and it keeps going,"

Before I could respond, Mic sat upright on the edge of the loveseat. *"Hey!"* they exclaimed, *"I think WE are the unicorn!"*

The Audacity of Queerness

In the face of today's global resurgence of white nationalism and the escalation of violence against marginalized peoples, the challenge—and importance—of storying queer resistance goes beyond the therapy room. It requires more from us than just queering our practice by diagnosing discourses and asking response-based questions.

Resisting the marginalization and oppression of queer and trans people and their families requires our constant attention to, and participation in, the world around us. Queer ethics demand that we become part of the fabric of the communities we work with. Indeed, the practice of queer theory-informed narrative therapy calls on us to *embody a particular worldview*, not just take up a set of techniques. When we leave our therapy offices, we don't stop asking questions; we don't stop interrogating power relations; and we don't stop deconstructing discourses. We have to take a stand. We have to have skin in the game. We have to *be the unicorn*.

This means working toward transformational change—that is, change that upends and transforms the existing rules, structures, and assumptions that maintain dominating systems and worldviews. Transformational change is also known as *second-order change*.

First-order change—that is, non-transformational change—offers modifications or adjustments *within* a particular context. For example, when a school establishes "safe spaces" and identifies "safe staff" for queer and trans students, but does not work to expose and dismantle the culture of homophobia, heteronormativity, transphobia, and cisnormativity that makes these spaces necessary—that is a first-order change. First-order change offers band-aids for bullet wounds: it may stop the bleeding and slow down the infection, but it doesn't change the culture behind the gunshot. First-order change involves new responses that nevertheless maintain (or allow) the same system within which we respond.

Transformational or second-order change involves the audacity to hope beyond what we know and believe, and to see past what is…to what could be. Thus, in the above example, instead of asking how schools can protect queer and trans students from the risks of homophobia, etc., we might instead ask: *How can we create safe and welcoming learning communities that see and hear all students, by working to make homophobia and transphobia things of the past?* This means that we also ask questions that move our attention (and action) from individuals and relationships to the discursive contexts that shape them.

Below are some more examples:

- Instead of asking *How do we support parents of queer youth when their children come out?* we might ask, *How do we create a world where parents understand that all sexual orientations and gender identities are emergent, fluid dimensions of peoples' experiences, thus eliminating the need to "come out"?*
- Instead of asking, *How can we increase the capacity of trans-competent therapists to write letters for gender confirmation services?* we might ask, *How do we de-medicalize, de-pathologize, and un-diagnose gender so that trans people have the authority to request and consent to the care they want, without getting permission slips from therapists or physicians? How do we provide and ensure health care for everyone?*
- Instead of asking, *What therapeutic practices can we use to help queer and trans people who are struggling with suicide stay safe?* we might ask, *What oppressive discourses and institutions must we dismantle so that no queer or trans person—or anyone else—feels that their life needs to end because of them?*

These questions, and their possible answers, reflect what critical pedagogue Jeffrey Duncan-Andrade (2009) calls *audacious hope*. This is opposed to false hope,[3] which is premised on individualism. Audacious hope requires us to imagine beyond the bounds of what we think is possible—but what is nevertheless necessary—for us to be truly free. According to

Duncan-Andrade, audacious hope "demands that we reconnect to the collective by struggling alongside one another, sharing in the victories *and* the pain" (p. 190).

Reconnecting to the collective demands that we erase many of the lines we draw between ourselves and others. Duncan-Andrade insists that there is no such thing as what Delpit (1995) refers to as "other people's children." In working with our therapy clients, we can erase many of these lines by queering conventional notions of therapy, therapists, and their relationships with clients.

Queering requires audacity. In this instance, it's the audacity to refuse the dehumanization of relationally distant and technique-centric therapy practices. It's also the audacity to co-create radical belonging with the people who consult us.

Queering also requires action. Like other critical liberatory educators before him (e.g., Freire, 1970, 1992; hooks, 1994, 2003), Duncan-Andrade is clear that hope requires action to be meaningful.

Let me add that *hope*, like *queer*, is at its best as a verb. Hoping leads to doing, and doing inspires and sustains hoping. Hoping is a praxis.

Think about Mic: they were feeling rather hope-less, until they saw the audacity (and queerness) of the planned community action. Once Mic saw the action as meaningful, their hope was re-invigorated; and, as Mic reconnected with hope, they felt inspired to act. Doing and hoping, hoping and doing....

Mic stepped into the praxis of hop(ing) because: (1) they saw a connection between themselves and trans youth in North Carolina (connection to the collective), (2) they resonated with the audacious queerness and queer audacity of the community response, and (3) they saw beyond *what was* to *what was possible*.

This may seem like hoping for Utopia (or Queertopia, as Mic and I called it in our conversations). Yet queerness is more than just audacious. Munoz (2009) contends that queerness *is* Utopian, and that "there is something queer about the utopian" (p. 170). Invoking the social poetics of possibility, Munoz tells us that "(q)ueerness is that thing that lets us feel that this world is not enough, that indeed something is missing" (p. 1).

Isn't that what hope is—an envisioning of, and reaching for, something other than what we are offered? For queer and trans people—as well as for all marginalized and oppressed people—imagining, hoping for, and working toward "something missing" are often literally a matter of life or death.

This is not an either/or proposition. I am not suggesting that we no longer work with parents when their children come out, or that we stop preparing more therapists to support trans people's pursuit of gender care. As long as those are needs, we must meet them. I *am*, however, advocating that we refuse to be satisfied with *only* meeting these needs, and that we ask different questions in order to make new, unique pathways possible.

We need to ask ourselves if it's enough if what we *do simply maintains the status quo.* That is, is it good enough if we help queer and trans people feel happier in a world where anti-queer and trans bias and violence are common? Is it good enough to train more therapists to write letters for trans people to get the medical services they need, while the system of expert-knows-best gatekeeping continues, and insurance companies increasingly call the shots? Queer theory, narrative therapy, and relational ethics teach me that it's not.

Taking these teachings to heart means that we persistently and queerly hope with audacity; that we imagine beyond what we're told is possible; and that we work to actively dismantle the discourses and systems that desperately try to keep things the same. And that is the critical part: audaciously hoping and queering are not merely aspirational abstractions; Munoz (2009) insists that "queerness…is not simply a being but a doing for and toward the future." Queerness rejects the here and now and demands the "concrete possibility of another world" (p. 1). This is core to the project of audacious hope and queerness: you have to believe it to make it something you can see, and you have to construct stories that you want to live.

The Road to Queertopia Is Paved with Dangerous Ideas

The project of storying queer resistance took a dramatic turn following the 2016 election. The very day after Donald Trump was declared the winner of the presidential race, much more palpable fear, despair, and desperation walked into my office with my clients. In the first several months after the election, I regularly had to do my own gut check to figure out where the fear, despair, and desperation that I was feeling started and ended, and where the fear, despair, and desperation gripping my clients began. All too often, this gut check revealed a concentric circle. As I write this chapter, roughly three and a half years since that fateful November night, I wouldn't say that my clients' responses have calmed or lessened. I would say, however, that people are also now angry—*righteously raging*—at the assaults on their dignity, and sometimes their lives. Together, we are leveraging that rage and honoring it as a declaration of dignity. We are protesting injustices that are baked into a system designed to oppress.

Storying queer resistance requires that we have a clear view of what we are constructing stories in *resistance to*. This involves having an awareness of the local, state, and federal political climate, and of the laws that impact queer and trans people in a variety of areas, including:

• Employment
• Child welfare
• Housing
• Adoption
• Conversion therapy
• School bullying
• Trans student athletes
• Hate crimes
• Gender markers on identification documents
• Public accommodations
• Education
• Transgender health care
• Minor consent to treatment.

Depending on your local jurisdiction, queer and trans people may experience varying degrees of *legal discrimination*.[4] It is incumbent on us as therapists to know not only the laws in our localities, but also where to refer people for legal support and advocacy. We also must see past our practice and work to transform the social and political landscape.

This is an ethical matter. If we understand that problems are located in the social world of discourse, and that people's personal narratives are influenced by this world, we must attend to what happens on this level.

As we've seen, queering our practice involves disrupting conventional ideas of professionalism and the limits of practice. Given the current urgency of our clients' situations, this is no time to be constrained by conventions. We need to traffic in dangerous ideas.

Dangerous ideas. These are the stones that pave the path to Queertopia. Dangerous ideas are both the map and the compass pointing to a new queer—and queering—territory. Dangerous ideas are the stuff of Mic's notion that people lining the streets of Minneapolis could change the conditions for trans people in North Carolina. This pathway of dangerous ideas leads us away from a landscape shaped and defined by the prevailing normative discourses we've discussed in this book, to the world of Mic's (and so many other's) imaginations.

I hope that when you read *We need to traffic in dangerous ideas*, your first question was, *Dangerous for whom? The answer is, Dangerous for the status quo; for discourses and institutions that are dangerous to queer and trans people; and for anyone who benefits from those discourses.*

Imagining beyond what we know, questioning taken-for-granted certainties, and hoping audaciously require us to take risks that push us out of our comfort zones—and may require personal sacrifices. Plan to make them.

We need dangerous ideas to create and sustain Queertopia. Queer theory-informed narrative therapy is one of those dangerous ideas. It offers the possibility of transformational change. It cuts a trail peppered with audacious hope toward newly imagined stories—as well as reclaimed stories of queerness. These stories center not on *individual* futures but on "a collective futurity" (Tilsen & Nylund, 2010).

You can play it safe, or you can work to make the world safe. What path will you take?

Notes

1. Mic is the 13-year-old non-binary young person you met in the Introduction.
2. "Bathroom bill" is the term commonly used to refer to legislation on access to public toilets based on gender. Some US states have proposed bills to prohibit trans people from using the bathroom that aligns with their gender identity.

3. Duncan-Andrade (2009) articulates three types of false hope: hokey hope, mythical hope, and hope deferred. Alternatively, he offers three types of *critical hope:* material hope, Socratic hope, and audacious hope.

4. For a comprehensive and frequently updated list of laws by state, go to the Human Rights Campaign issues maps: https://www.hrc.org/state-maps.

Appendix

SAMPLE NARRATIVE THERAPY COUNTER DOCUMENTS

Narrative therapists use a variety of counter documents. Here are some examples from my practice. (The names and details have been changed to protect confidentiality.)

Sample Between-Session Letter or E-mail

Dear Puck,

Of course, after you left yesterday, I thought of a couple of questions that I wish I had thought of while we were meeting. We both got pretty caught up in the discussion about how you "took care of myself at the gender doctor" and I just never got around to asking more about what you said about your visit last week with your grandparents.

So, here are a couple of questions...better late than never? I hope these questions are useful for you—no worries if they're not. I'll be interested to hear what you think when we meet next time.

Puck, you said, "I don't feel like I need to push my 75-year-old, farm-town grandparents too hard to use they/them pronouns. That's not how I want to spend the time I get with them, correcting them or feeling mad at them." Puck, given how hard you've advocated for yourself and for people to respect your identity, what does your not needing to "push too hard" say about your relationship with your grandparents? How have your efforts to be "good in my gender and who I am" prepared you to "give a little for them"? What are you hoping will come from this "giving a little" for you and your relationship?

Puck, I look forward to our next conversation.

Not pushing ☺,
Julie

Sample Gender Euphoria Letter or E-mail

To Whom It May Concern,

I am writing this letter as a witness to Wren's gender journey and to participate in the documenting of "the joy and liberation" she feels as she prepares for gender affirmation surgery.

Wren is grateful to "the little kid in me who refused to follow the rules of gender" even when that was hard. She remembers fondly how, at age 12, she "just matter-of-factly told mom and dad, hey, guys, you got it wrong. I'm a girl!" Wren believes that her younger self kept the vision she is "now able to realize and experience" alive by being "careful and smart, keeping myself safe."

Wren says that as a young teenager, she "found my fierceness," standing up to gender expectations and the people who tried to bully her into following them. She also says that this fierceness "helped me literally stay alive when dysphoria was really strong." Wren says that she "saw a light at the end of the tunnel" when she met other trans youth online and "knew that who I am is real." When she met other trans students in real life during her sophomore year in high school, Wren says, "I was unstoppable once I had people around me."

Wren is clear that the "joy and liberation" she experiences is not only because she is living into her identity and has important people who honor and respect her, but also because "this experience has led me to learn so much about myself and other people." Wren has plans to share her experience with, and knowledge about, gender identity with other young "gender outlaws."

In solidarity,
Julie

Sample Invitation Letter or Email for Letter Writing Campaign

Dear Friends and Family of Taj:

My name is Julie Tilsen and Taj has asked me to contact you to invite your support. Specifically, Taj would like your assistance as she stands up to Homophobia and, in particular, the ways it has brought Self-Doubt, Fear, and Substance Mis-use into her life. Taj is actively resisting these problems so that she can continue on her Reclaiming her Best Self Project. She has specifically selected you as a member of her support team.

You may be aware that Taj has been struggling with these problems intermittently for a few years. What you may not know is that the impact of these problems, coupled with the stressors of a move to a new city, have left Taj a captive of Self-Doubt, Fear, and Substance Misuse. Currently, this triumvirate of trouble is really bossing her around. It's probably hard for you to believe this—some of the messages these problems push on Taj include that she "doesn't deserve to be loved," that she "isn't enough," and that she "isn't capable."

Because of the powerful influence of these problems, Taj and I are asking your support in helping her resist their propaganda so that she may continue on her Reclaiming her Best Self Project. Taj believes (as do I) that as her found family you can help her take back her life from the despair of these problems.

Here's what we're asking you do to: Please send Taj a brief letter expressing (1) how you remember your history with her—your favorite stories, what you admire and appreciate about who she is in relationship to you; (2) your thoughts and feeling about her resistance to these problems, and what that says about who she is in the present; and (3) how you believe you would like to see your relationship with Taj be in the future.

Taj has also said that it's important that you know this: this is *not* an emergency and she is *not* asking that you contact her with advice. She has chosen you to participate in this campaign because she anticipates your stories of the past and future will help her acts of resistance in the present lead to her reclamation of her best self.

We hope that your letters of support are not too much to ask, and we want you to know that they will be greatly appreciated. Taj would like all of you to know that she will respond to your replies.

Warm Regards,

Julie Tilsen, MA, LP, PhD

Project Consultant

Sample Award Certificates

☆ STANDING UP TO TEASING CERTIFICATE ☆

AWARDED TO

☆☆☆ **COLE** ☆☆☆

☆ *For standing up to teasing and standing for what's right.* ☆

COLE would like everyone to know that homophobia is not your friend and that friends don't tease you.

COLE is prepared to teach you how to stand up to teasing and how to be a good friend.

COLE will help you remember that some kids have 2 moms or 2 dads.

_____   _____
Signed   Date

CERTIFICATE of
Supportive Parenting
This certifies that
Terri & Nathan (AKA, "Mom & Dad")
Have successfully completed their training in
supportive parenting of queer youth
at the Institute of Parent-offspring Solidarity

_____   _____
Offspring   Date

REFERENCES

American Association for Marriage and Family Therapy. (January 2015). *Code of ethics*. Retrieved from https://www.aamft.org/Legal_Ethics/Code_of_Ethics.aspx.

American Psychiatric Association. (2013). DSM-5: *Diagnostic and statistical manual for mental disorders*. (5th ed.). Washington, DC: American Psychiatric Press.

American Psychological Association. (June 2003). *Ethical principles of psychologists and code of conduct*. Retrieved from https://www.apa.org/ethics/code

Anzaldúa, G. (1987). *Borderlands/La Frontera: The new mestiza*. San Francisco, CA: Aunt Lute.

Anzaldúa, G. (1991). To(o) Queer the writer: loca, escrita y chicana. In Warland (Ed.), *InVersions: Writing by dykes, queers, and lesbians* (pp. 249–263). Vancouver: Press Gang.

Bakhtin, M. M. (1981). *The dialogic imagination: Four essays*. Ed. Michael Holquist. Trans. Caryl Emerson and Michael Holquist. Austin and London: University of Texas Press.

Barker, M. J. (2012). Retrieved from https://www.rewriting-the-rules.com/sex/sex-critical/

Barker, M. J., & Hancock, J. (2017). *Enjoy sex: How, when and IF you want to*. London: Icon Books.

Barnard, I. (1999). Queer race. *Social Semantics, 9*(2), 199–212.

Bateson, G. (1972). *Steps to an ecology of the mind: Collected essays in anthropology, psychiatry, evolution, and epistemology.* Chicago, IL: University of Chicago Press.

Bateson, G. (1979). *Mind and nature: A necessary unity.* New York: Dutton.

Bavelas, J. B., Coates, L., & Johnson, T. (2000). Listeners as co-narrators. *Journal of Personality and Social Psychology, 79*(6), 941–952.

Beckett, S. (2007). Azima ila Hayati –An invitation into my life: Narrative conversations about sexual identity. *International Journal of Narrative Therapy and Community Work, 1,* 29–39.

Bjoroy, A., Madigan, S., & Nylund, D. (2015). The practice of therapeutic letter writing in narrative therapy. In B. Douglas, R. Woolfe, S. Strawbridge, E. Kasket, & V. Galbraith (Eds.), *The handbook of counselling psychology* (4th ed., pp. 332–348. London: Sage.

Blank, H. (2012). *Straight: The surprisingly short history of heterosexuality.* Boston, MA: Beacon, Press.

Buder, E. (2018). Couples speak honestly about open relationships. *The Atlantic.* Retrieved from https://www.theatlantic.com/video/index/556988/open-relationship-nonmonogamy/

Bull, B., & D'Arrigo-Patrick, J. (2018). Parent experiences of a child's social transition: Moving beyond the loss narrative. *Journal of Feminist Family Therapy, 30*(3), 170–190.

Butler, J. (1990). *Gender trouble: Gender and the subversion of identity.* New York: Routledge.

Butler, J. (1993). *Bodies that matter: On the discursive limits of "sex".* New York: Routledge.

Carey, M., & Russel, S. (2002). Externalising: Commonly-asked questions. *International Journal of Narrative Therapy and Community Work, 2,* 76–84.

Carey, M., Walter, S., & Russel, S. (2009). The absent but implicit: A map to support therapeutic inquiry. *Family Process, 48*(3), 319–331.

Cass, V. C. (1984). Homosexual identity formation: Testing a theoretical model. *Journal of Sex Research, 20*(2), 210–235.

Coates, L., & Wade, A. (2007). Language and violence: Analysis of four discursive operations. *Journal of Family Violence, 22*(7), 511–522.

Coleman, E. (1981/1982). Developmental stages of the coming out process. *Journal of Homosexuality, 7*(2–3), 31–43.

Collins, P.H. (2009). Foreword: Emerging intersections—Building knowledge and transforming institutions. In B. Thornton Dill & R. Enid (Eds.), *Emerging Intersections: Race, Class, and Gender in Theory, Policy, and Practice* (pp. vii–xiii). New Brunswick, NJ: Rutgers University Press.

Collins, P.H. (2015). Intersectionality: Definitional dilemmas. *Annual Review of Sociology, 4*(1), 1–20.

Combs, G., & Freedman, J. (2012). Narrative, poststructuralism, and social justice: Current practices in narrative therapy. *The Counseling Psychologist, 40*(7), 1033–1060.

Crenshaw, K. (1993). Beyond racism and misogyny: Black feminism and 2 Live Crew. In M. J. Matsuda, C. R. Lawrence, III, R. Delgado, & K. W. Crenshaw (Eds.), *Words that wound: Critical race theory, assaultive speech, and the first amendment* (pp. 111–132). Boulder, CO: Westview Press.

Cushman, P. (1995). *Constructing the self, constructing America: A cultural history of psychotherapy*. Boston, MA: Da Capo Press.

de Lauretis, T. (1991). Queer theory: Lesbian and gay sexualities. *Differences: A Journal of Feminist Cultural Studies, 3*(2), 296–313.

Delpit, L. (1995). *Other people's children*. New York: New Press.

Denborough, D. (2014). *Retelling the stories of our lives: Every day narrative therapy to draw inspiration and transform experience*. New York: W.W. Norton.

Derrida, J. (1967). *Of grammatology*. Baltimore, MD: John Hopkins University Press.

Derrida, J. (1977). *Limited, Inc.* Evanston, IL: Northwestern University Press.

de Shazer, S. (1994). *Words were originally magic*. New York: W.W. Norton.

deVries, G. (2008). Unsuitable for children. In M. B. Sycamore (Ed.), *That's revolting! Queer strategies for resisting assimilation (rev)* (pp. 141–146). Brooklyn, NY: Soft Skull Press.

Dietz, C., & Thompson, J. (2004). Rethinking boundaries: Ethical dilemmas in the social worker-client relationship. *Journal of Progressive Human Services, 15*(2), 1–24.

Dominus, S. (2017). Is an open marriage a happier marriage? *New York Times.* Retrieved from https://www.nytimes.com/2017/05/11/magazine/is-an-open-marriage-a-happier marriage.html

Doty, A. (1993). *Making things perfectly queer: Interpreting mass culture.* Minneapolis: University of Minnesota Press.

Downing, L. (2012). Safewording! Kinkphobia and gender normativity in *Fifty Shades of Grey*. *Psychology and Sexuality, 4*(1), 92–102.

Duggan, L. (2002). *The incredible shrinking public: Sexual politics and the decline of democracy*. Boston, MA: Beacon Press.

Duncan-Andrade, J. M. R. (2009). Note to educators: Hope required when growing roses in concrete. *Harvard Educational Review, 79*(2), 181–194.

Engle, G. (2019). The ultimate guide to making an open relationship work. Men's Health. Retrieved from https://www.menshealth.com/sex-women/a26111265/open-relationship-guide/

Everett, B., MacFarlane, D. A., Reynolds, V. A., & Anderson, H. D. (2013). Not on our backs: Supporting counsellors in navigating the ethics of multiple relationships within queer, Two Spirit, and/or trans communities. *Canadian Journal of Counselling and Psychotherapy, 47*(1), 14–28.

Ferguson, R. A. (2019). *One dimensional queer*. Medford, MA: Polity Press.

Fisher, M. (2009). *Capitalist realism: Is there no alternative?* Alresford: Zero Books.

Flaskas, C., McCarthy, I., & Sheehan, J. (Eds.). (2007). *Hope and despair in narrative and family therapy*. New York: Routledge.

Foucault, M. (1965). *Madness and civilization: A history of insanity in the age of reason*. Trans. R. Howard. New York: Random House.

Foucault, M. (1970). *The order of things: An archeology of human sciences*. New York: Pantheon (original work published in 1966).

Foucault, M. (1975). *The birth of the clinic: An archeology of medical perception*. Trans. A. M. Sheridan Smith. New York: Random House.

Foucault, M. (1977). *Discipline and punish: The birth of the prison*. Trans. A. Sheridan. New York: Pantheon Books.

Foucault, M. (1978). *The history of sexuality, Vol. 1: An introduction*. New York: Pantheon (original work published in 1976).

Foucault, M. (1985). *History of sexuality, Vol. 2: The use of pleasure*. Trans. R. Hurley. New York: Pantheon Books.

Foucault, M. (1997). The ethics of the concern of the self as a practice of freedom: Interview with H. Becker, R. Fornet-Betancourt, & A. Gomez-Miller, 1984. In P. Rabinow (Ed.), *Ethics, subjectivity and truth: The essential works of Foucault 1954–1984. Vol. 1* (pp. 281–301). New York: The New Press.

Freedman, J. (2012). Explorations of the absent but implicit. *International Journal of Narrative Therapy and Community Work, 4*, 1–10.

Freedman, J., & Combs, G. (1996). *Narrative therapy: The social construction of preferred realities.* New York: Norton.

Freire, P. (1970). *Pedagogy of the oppressed.* New York: Continuum.

Freire, P. (1992). *Pedagogy of hope.* New York: Continuum.

Freud, S. (1959). *The question of lay analysis.* New York: Norton (original work published in 1926).

Geertz, C. (1976). "From the native's point of view": On the nature of anthropological understanding. In K. Basso & H. Selby (Eds.), *Meaning in anthropology* (pp. 221–237). Albuquerque: University of New Mexico Press.

Gopinath, G. (2005). *Impossible desires: Queer diasporas and South Asian public cultures.* Durham, NC: Duke University Press.

Greenspan, M. (1995). Out of bounds. *Common Boundary,* July/August, 51–58.

Halberstam, J. (1998). *Female masculinities.* Durham, NC: Duke University Press.

Halberstam, J. (2005). *In a queer time and place: Transgender bodies, subcultural lives.* New York: NYU Press.

Halberstam, J. (2011). *The queer art of failure.* Durham, NC: Duke University Press.

Hedtke, L., & Windsalde, J. (2005). The use of the subjunctive in re-membering conversations with those who are grieving. *Omega,* 50(3), 197–215.

Hedtke, L., & Winslade, J. (2017). *The crafting of grief: Aesthetic responses to loss.* New York: Routledge.

Heinz, M. (2012). Transmen on the web: Inscribing multiple discourses. In Karen Ross (Ed.), *The handbook of gender, sex, and media* (pp. 326–343). Hoboken, NJ: Wiley.

Hill, M., Glaser, K., & Harden, J. (1998). A feminist model for ethical decision making. *Women & Therapy,* 21(3), 101–121.

hooks, b. (1994). *Teaching to transgress: Education as the practice of freedom.* New York: Routledge.

hooks, b. (2001). *All about love: New visions.* New York: William Morrow.

hooks, b. (2003). *Teaching community: A pedagogy of hope.* New York: Routledge.

hooks, b. (2014) [1984]. *Feminist theory: From margin to center* (3rd ed.). New York: Routledge.

Iantaffi, A., & Barker, M. J. (2018). *How to understand your gender: A practical guide for exploring who you are.* London: Jessica Kingsley Publishers.

James, O. (2008). *The selfish capitalist.* London: Vermilion.

Jenkins, A. (1990). *Invitations to responsibility: The therapeutic engagement of men who are violent and abusive.* Adelaide: Dulwich Centre Publications.

Jones, A. (2018). What were her knickers like? The truth about trying an open relationship. *The Guardian.* Retrieved from https://www.theguardian.com/lifeandstyle/2018/sep/08/knickers-truthabout-trying-open-relationship

Jones, R. P., & Cox, D. (2015). *How race and religion shape millennial attitudes on sexuality and reproductive health findings from the 2015 millennials, sexuality, and reproductive health survey.* Washington, DC: Public Religion Research Institute.

Jordan, J. V. (1991). Empathy and self-boundaries. In J. V. Jordan, A. G. Kaplan, J. B. Miller, I. P. Stiver, and J. L. Surrey (Eds.), *Women's growth in connection* (pp. 67–80). New York: Guilford Press.

Jordan, J. V. (1997). Relational therapy in a nonrelational world. *Work in Progress,* 79. Wellesley, MA: The Stone Center.

King, Deborah K. (1988). Multiple jeopardy, multiple consciousness: The context of a black feminist ideology. *Signs, 14*(1), 42–72.

Kosciw, J. G., Greytak, E. A., Palmer, N. A., & Boesen, M. J. (2014). *The 2013 National School Climate Survey: The experiences of lesbian, gay, bisexual and transgender youth in our nation's schools.* New York: GLSEN.

LaMarre, A., Smoliak, O., Cool, C., Kinavey, H., & Hardt, L. (2018). The normal, improving, and productive self: Unpacking neoliberal governmentality in therapeutic interactions. *Journal of Constructivist Psychology, 32*(3), 236–253.

Lazarus, A. A., & Zur, O. (2002). Six arguments against dual relationships and their rebuttals. In A. A. Lazarus & O. Zur (Eds.), *Dual relationships and psychotherapy* (pp. 3–24). New York: Springer Publishing.

MacFarlane, D. (2003). *LGBT communities and substance use: What health has to do with it!* Vancouver: LGBT Health Association.

MacFarlane, D., Everett, B., Marlow, M., Hutchings, A., Spicer, B., Clifford, D., ... Barlow, R. (2010). *Multiple relationships: Establishing professional relationships and maintaining appropriate boundaries when working with clientele from small and or marginalized communities.* Unpublished document, Vancouver Coastal Health, Vancouver, BC.

Madigan, S. (2011). *Narrative therapy.* Washington, DC: APA.

Madsen, W. C. (2007). *Collaborative therapy with multi-stressed families* (2nd ed.). New York: Guilford.

Martin, K. A., Hutson, D. J., Kazyak, E., & Scherrer, K. S. (2010). Advice when children come out: The cultural "tool kits" of parents. *Journal of Family Issues, 31*(7), 960–991.

McNamee, S. (2009). Postmodern psychotherapeutic ethics: Relational responsibility in practice. *Human Systems 20*(2), 55-69.

McNamee, S. (2015). Ethics as discursive potential. *Australian and New Zealand Journal of Family Therapy, 36*(4), 419–433.

Mercer, K. (1994). *Welcome to the jungle: New positions in black cultural studies*. New York: Routledge.

Moraga, C. (1996). Queer Aztlán: The reformation of Chicano tribe. In D. Morton (Ed.), *The material queer: A LesBiGay cultural studies reader* (pp. 297–304). Boulder, CO: Westview Press.

Morgan, A. (2000). *What is narrative therapy?* Adelaide: Dulwich Centre Publications.

Munoz, J. E. (2009). *Cruising Utopia: The then and there of queer futurity*. New York: NYU Press.

Namaste, K. (1996). Tragic misreadings: Queer theory's erasure of transgender subjectivity. In B. Beemyn & M. Eliason (Eds.), *Queer studies: A lesbian, gay, bisexual and transgender anthology* (pp. 183–203). New York: New York University Press.

National Association of Social Workers. (2017). *Code of ethics*. Retrieved from https://www.socialworkers.org/about/ethics/code-of-ethics/code-of-ethics-english

Norwood, K. (2012). Grieving gender: Trans-identities, transition, and ambiguous loss. *Communication Monographs, 80*(1), 24–45.

Nylund, D. (2000). *Treating Huckleberry Finn: A new narrative approach with kids diagnosed ADD/ADHD*. San Francisco, CA: Jossey-Bass.

Peterson, M. R. (1992). *At personal risk: Boundary violations in professional-client relationships*. New York: W.W. Norton.

Reynolds, V. (2010). A supervision of solidarity. *Canadian Journal of Counselling, 44*(3), 246–257.

Richardson, C. (2015). The role of response-based practice in activism. In M. Hyden, D. Gadd, & A. Wade (Eds.), *Response-based Approaches to the Study of Interpersonal Violence* (pp. 196–215). London, UK: Palgrave MacMillan.

Rubin, G. (1984). Thinking sex: Notes for a radical theory of the politics of sexuality. In C. S. Vance (Ed.), *Pleasures and danger: Exploring female sexuality* (pp. 267–319). Boston, MA: Routledge.

Savin-Williams, R. (1998). ...And then I became gay: Young men's stories. New York: Routledge.

Savin-Williams, R., & Diamond, L. (1997). Sexual orientation as a developmental context for lesbians, gays, and bisexuals: Biological perspectives. In N. L. Segal, G. E., Weisfeld, & C. C. Weisfeld (Eds.), Uniting psychology and biology: Integrative perspectives on human development (pp. 217–238). Washington, DC: APA Press.

Schalet, A. (2011). Not under my roof: Teens, parents, and the culture of sex. Chicago, IL: University of Chicago Press.

Sedgewick, E. (1990). Epistemology of the closet. Berkley: University of California Press.

Sedgewick, E. (1993). Tendencies. Durham, NC: Duke University Press.

Strong, T., & Zeman, D. (2005). 'Othering' and 'selving' in therapeutic dialogue. European Journal of Psychotherapy and Counseling, 7(4), 245–261.

Sullivan, N. (2003). A critical introduction to queer theory. New York: New York University Press.

Tiefer, L. (2004). Sex is not a natural act and other essays. New York: Routledge.

Tilsen, J. (2010). Resisting homonormativity: Therapeutic conversations with queer youth. (Unpublished doctoral dissertation). Tilburg University, Tilburg, The Netherlands.

Tilsen, J. (2013). Therapeutic conversations with queer youth: Transcending homonormativity and constructing preferred identities. Lanham, MD: Rowman and Littlefield.

Tilsen, J. (2018). Narrative approaches to youth work: Conversational skills for a critical practice. New York: Routledge.

Tilsen, J., & Nylund, D. (2010). Resisting normativity: Queer musings on politics, identity, and the performance of therapy. International Journal of Narrative Therapy and Community Work, 3, 66–72.

Tomm, K. (1993). The ethics of dual relationships. The California Therapist, January/February, 7–9.

Travers, A. (2018). The trans generation: How trans kids (and their parents) are creating a gender revolution. New York: New York University Press.

Troiden, R. R. (1979). Becoming homosexual: A model of identity acquisition. Psychiatry, 42, 288–299.

Vincenty, S. (2019). What to know about open relationships. The Oprah Magazine. Retrieved from https://www.oprahmag.com/life/relationships-love/a29643939/open-relationshipmeaning/

Wade, A. (1997). Small acts of living. *Contemporary Family Therapy, 19*(1), 23–39.

Warner, M. (1991). Introduction: Fear of a queer planet. *Social Text, 9*, 3–17.

Warner, M. (Ed.). (1993). *Fear of a queer planet*. Minneapolis: University of Minnesota Press.

Warner, M. (1999). *The trouble with normal: Sex, politics, and the ethics of queer life*. Cambridge, MA: Harvard University Press.

White, J. (2007). Knowing, doing, and being in context: A praxis-oriented approach to child and youth care. *Child and Youth Care Forum, 36*, 225–244.

White, J., & Morris, J. (2019). Re-thinking ethics and politics in suicide prevention: Bringing narrative ideas into dialogue with critical suicide studies. *International Journal of Environmental Research and Public Health, 16*(18), article #3236; no page number.

White, M. (1997). *Narratives of therapists' lives*. Adelaide: Dulwich Centre Publications.

White, M. (2000). *Reflections on narrative practice: Essays and interviews*. Adelaide: Dulwich Centre Publications.

White, M. (2007). *Maps of narrative practice*. New York: Norton.

White, M., & Epston, D. (1990). *Narrative means to therapeutic ends*. New York: Norton.

Williams, A. (2017). Is an open relationship right for you? *Huffpost*. Retrieved from https://www.huffpost.com/entry/open-relationship-right-for-you_n_5a09e371e4b00a6eece343ef

Winslade. J. (2009). Tracing lines of flight: Implications of the work of Gilles Deleuze for narrative practice. *Family Process, 48*(3), 332–346.

Wittgenstein, L. (1953). *Philosophical investigations*. Oxford: Blackwell.

Zur, O. (2000a). In celebration of dual relationships: How prohibition of non-sexual dual relationships increases the chance of exploitation and harm. *Independent Practitioner, 2*(3), 97–100.

Zur, O. (2000b). Going too far in the right direction: Reflections on the mythic ban of dual relationships. *The California Psychologist, 23*(4), 14–16.

Zur, O. (2001). Out-of-office experience: When crossing office boundaries and engaging in dual relationships are clinically beneficial and ethically sound. *Independent Practitioner, 21*(1), 96–100.

INDEX

Note: Page numbers followed by "n" denote endnotes.